UNIPA Springer Series

The **UNIPA Springer Series** publishes single and co-authored thematic collected volumes, monographs, handbooks and advanced textbooks, conference proceedings, professional books, SpringerBriefs, journals on specific issues of particular relevance in six core scientific areas. The issues may be interdisciplinary or within one specific area of interest. Manuscripts are invited for publication in the following fields of study:

1- Clinical Medicine;
2- Biomedical and Life Sciences;
3- Engineering and Physical Sciences;
4- Mathematics, Statistics and Computer Science;
5- Business, Economics and Law;
6- Human, Behavioral and Social Sciences.

Manuscripts submitted to the series are peer reviewed for scientific rigor followed by the usual Springer standards of editing, production, marketing and distribution. The series will allow authors to showcase their research within the context of a dynamic multidisciplinary platform. The series is open to academics from the University of Palermo but also from other universities around the world. Both scientific and teaching contributions are welcome in this series. The editorial products are addressed to researchers and students and will be published in the English language.

More information about this series at http://www.springer.com/series/13175

Guido Smorto · Ignazio Vinci
Editors

The Role of Sharing Mobility in Contemporary Cities

Legal, Social and Environmental Issues

With the support of the Erasmus+ Programme

UNIVERSITÀ DEGLI STUDI DI PALERMO

Springer

Editors
Guido Smorto
Dipartimento di Giurisprudenza
University of Palermo
Palermo, Italy

Ignazio Vinci
Dipartimento di Architettura
University of Palermo
Palermo, Italy

ISSN 2366-7516 ISSN 2366-7524 (electronic)
UNIPA Springer Series
ISBN 978-3-030-57724-7 ISBN 978-3-030-57725-4 (eBook)
https://doi.org/10.1007/978-3-030-57725-4

This Springer imprint is published by the registered company Springer Nature Switzerland AG
The registered company address is: Gewerbestrasse 11, 6330 Cham, Switzerland

Contents

Editors and Contributors

About the Editors

Guido Smorto is Full Professor of Comparative Law at the University of Palermo, Department of Law.

Ignazio Vinci is Associate Professor of Urban Planning at the University of Palermo, Department of Architecture.

Contributors

Sofia Asperti is Research Associate at the Sustainable Mobility Unit of the Sustainable Development Foundation (Italy).

Patrícia Baptista is Researcher at the Center for Innovation, Technology and Policy Research, Universidade de Lisboa.

Massimo Ciuffini is Head of the Sustainable Mobility Unit at the Sustainable Development Foundation (Italy).

Martina Di Marco is Research Fellow at the University of Palermo, Department of Psychological, Educational and Training Sciences.

Cristiano Inguglia is Associate Professor of Developmental and Educational Psychology at the University of Palermo, Department of Psychological, Educational and Training Sciences.

Luca Refrigeri is Research Associate at the Sustainable Mobility Unit of the Sustainable Development Foundation (Italy).

Miriam Ricci is Senior Research Fellow at the University of the West of England, Center for Transport and Society.

Catarina Rolim is Doctorate Researcher at the Center for Innovation, Technology and Policy Research, Universidade de Lisboa.

Joana Vicente is Researcher at the Center for Innovation, Technology and Policy Research, Universidade de Lisboa.

A Multidisciplinary Approach to Sharing Mobility: An Introduction

Guido Smorto and Ignazio Vinci

Abstract This chapter introduces the book by explaining why a multidisciplinary approach is especially needed to appreciate the multifaceted impact of sharing mobility in contemporary urban areas. The spread of innovative mobility services based on sharing and digital technologies is deeply intertwined, inter alia, with environmental sustainability, urban organization and social inclusion, and it raises critical legal issues. The chapter ends with a short description of its constitutive sections and their respective achievements.

Keywords Sharing mobility · Regulation · Urban development · Environmental sustainability · Social inclusion

This book is part of an EU-funded project aimed at investigating the competing and sometimes diverging features that should be pondered in regulating (and deregulating) sharing mobility in Europe[1]. The objective of the project is to deepen understanding of the benefits and drawbacks of the many innovative mobility services based on sharing and digital technologies that are taking place in our cities, in order to recognise how to effectively seize the opportunities they offer[2].

Such an inquiry has revealed especially challenging for at least three reasons. First of all, 'sharing' (or 'shared') mobility is an indefinite and ill-defined subject. Despite the fact that the term has come into wide use, it is extensively employed by scholars and public authorities, and it is still a vague and polysemic expression. Sharing mobility is commonly described as part of the so-called sharing economy—sometimes also referred to as 'collaborative economy', 'collaborative consumption', 'access-based consumption' and so on—a similarly loose concept, as it encompasses a number of business models and operational characteristics. In a nutshell, it is

G. Smorto (✉)
Department of Law, University of Palermo, Palermo, Italy
e-mail: guido.smorto@unipa.it

I. Vinci
Department of Architecture, University of Palermo, Palermo, Italy
e-mail: ignazio.vinci@unipa.it

G. Smorto and I. Vinci (eds.), *The Role of Sharing Mobility in Contemporary Cities*, UNIPA Springer Series, https://doi.org/10.1007/978-3-030-57725-4_1

possible to pinpoint two basic features of the sharing economy (and mobility): the sharing of an asset instead of owning it and the reliance of these innovative services on technology. The core idea of the sharing economy is turning idle or underused assets into productive resources by sharing instead of owning them, thanks to technology—apps, the Internet, smartphones—that connects users and providers.

Mobility is perhaps the economic sector that has been most strongly affected by the sharing revolution. After all, being parked for most of their life cycle, and when used being often occupied only by the driver, automobiles and other privately owned vehicles are possibly the most striking pool of underutilised capital existing in the world. Sharing is not an entirely new idea in transportation. Both private and public mass transportation services have always allowed customers to temporarily access a vehicle together with other passengers. With regard to this, it is worth noting that the old idea of sharing a private car in a community has re-emerged with the rise of Internet and smartphone technology. Yet, until recently most slack resources could not be fully exploited to offer transport services, due to the difficulties traditionally involved in large-scale borrowing and lending. As a result, opportunities to share assets for the offering of transport services were severely limited by high transaction costs connected with enabling the shared use of resources. What differentiates new sharing mobility services from conventional ones is the use of information technology that enables new and far-reaching ways of sharing. The evolution from the first experiments in small communities that organised the private shared use of vehicles, to an effective business model based on vehicle sharing is mostly due to technological evolution. Internet, GPS, smartphones and related technologies have lowered transaction costs, so that the ties between consumption and ownership are loosening. Thanks to digital technologies, we can now tap into the spare capacity of many underutilised assets and deliver innovative services based on the shared use of resources.

Like sharing economy, the expression 'sharing mobility' also identifies a diverse range of innovative transport services that combine the benefits of consuming without the costs of ownership. This first broad definition of mobility embraces a large array of economic models: a wide range of services are commonly grouped as sharing mobility, making an overall analysis of the subject extremely difficult, as each of these models poses distinctive societal and legal challenges.

Firstly, the term sharing mobility designates those economic models based on short-term rental of vehicles, managed and owned by a public or private provider. The most prominent example of these sharing mobility services is perhaps car sharing, with providers that rent out their cars to customers, offering their users access to a dedicated fleet of vehicles that are owned or leased by the operator itself. Similarly, technological innovation has fostered bike sharing programs in much the same way.

What makes these new services dissimilar from traditional rentals is the enhanced possibility offered by technology to use the shared vehicle autonomously and whenever needed, allowing customers to use a shared vehicle as easily and immediately as a private one. Commonly, these operators have a number of vehicles parked in the most strategic areas of a city, so that users can look for a vehicle in a convenient location, use the car to drive to their destination and return the car at the end of the trip. Technology helps to make the user experience smooth: websites and apps help the user to reserve and to find a vehicle by tracking its location and availability, to lock and unlock it and to pay for the trip.

In addition to this first model, sharing mobility also encompasses other innovative services that employ digital technologies to enable the exchange of goods and the supply of services by a decentralised ‘crowd’ of individuals. This second model of sharing mobility services is based on vehicles owned by private individuals, usually organised by an app-based platform, which offers privately owned vehicles for rent, made temporarily available for shared use. This form of sharing involves using similar information technology to facilitate transactions between vehicle owners and people who would like to use those vehicles for short periods of time. Unlike the first model, here the provision of mobility services is facilitated by online intermediaries that help to connect people who own underutilised assets to people who are willing to pay to rent them. These digital intermediaries are said to provide a ‘marketplace’ to enable the supply of mobility services to the public by a decentralised ‘crowd’ of individuals, making it easier for providers and customers to find each other swiftly. An organisation or a company provides an online platform, such as a website or an app, for the coordination of supply and demand by offering their customers, both the owner and the user of the vehicle, an online search, a reservation tool, a contract and insurance. The platform usually collects the payment and takes a percentage of the total income. Such a service is sometimes defined as ‘peer to peer’, since it is provided by private, non-professional individuals who rent their cars when not in use. In some cases, this sharing of private cars is limited to neighbours or to closed community groups, with a cost-based business model.

Another remarkable model, often referred to as ride haring, is the provision of mobility services with companies that own no cars themselves, but they sign up ordinary car owners who act as drivers. The service operates in a taxi-like fashion, and relies on an app provided by the company, which also collects payment, and takes a percentage of the total income. In other cases, the service is based on on-demand private cars and other vehicles, shared by passengers going in the same direction. Sometimes, these services include the possibility to specify pick-up and drop-off locations and/or departure and/or arrival times, making them akin to shared taxi services, and taxi-bus services, with predetermined stops and reservation required in advance. Another variation of this model, used for long-distance travels, is based on drivers offering rides from one city to another to passengers willing to car pool. Companies, such as Uber, Lyft or BlaBlaCar, are the most prominent examples of this innovative business model.

Finally, sharing mobility is often assimilated to other innovative forms of transport, such as ‘micromobility’ services: a term commonly employed to designate personal transportation based on vehicles with reduced power supply and limited speed limit that include both human-powered vehicles, such as bicycles, skates and kick-scooters, as well as energy-powered vehicles. Despite being very different from the sharing mobility services described so far, micromobility is often included in the picture of sharing mobility as it can support existing sustainable mobility policies, and it also contributes to changing how people move by serving a previously unmet demand for point-to-point travel. As for sharing mobility, it can improve traffic safety by reducing the number of car and motorbikes trips, also offering a convenient door-to-door transport solution. Like sharing mobility, micromobility brings new and pressing challenges for policy-makers and city officials.

Besides being an indefinite subject, a second and significant difficulty in dealing with sharing mobility is its cross-cutting feature. And an in-depth investigation on sharing mobility does require a truly interdisciplinary approach together with a painstaking, wide-ranging dialogue among different disciplines. Market regulation is the most striking aspect of defining a suitable legal framework for sharing mobility. Sharing mobility calls into question consumer protection, antitrust laws, labour law, local regulations, and many other legal fields, making a wide-ranging legal analysis of the subject quite intricate. Many EU jurisdictions have amended their sectoral regulations, revisiting issues such as licensing, background checks, insurance, vehicle markings, geographical restrictions and the use of data. The result has often been a vast landscape of legal, commercial and political conflict, as well as normative chaos.

However, the case for regulating sharing mobility is not just a matter of market regulation and of fine-tuning appropriate rules for digital intermediaries and individual service providers. Sharing mobility has a significant impact on many aspects of our society, well beyond efficiency and market failures: environmental sustainability, urban planning, migration policies and social inclusion are just some of the most pressing aspects of the new mobility services. Its distributive impact is also crucial for a sound regulation. Mobility is vital to people's lives, and lack of transport services may hamper opportunities, determine social exclusion and cause economic hardship. In this regard, sharing mobility is often questioned, as in most cases it is still considered an exclusive program for middle-income, young white populations. There is a growing literature on the relationships between social exclusion and transport. Many studies show a strong correlation between a lack of access to adequate mobility and lack of access to opportunities, social networks, goods and services. A growing concern is expressed about the social exclusion of low-income groups and communities. Adopting a social exclusion approach to transport planning—by investigating the connections between poverty, transport disadvantage, access to key services and economic and social exclusion—may open up new avenues of research and help to identify new theoretical perspectives and methodological approaches.

Environmental sustainability is also at stake. In principle, shared use of vehicles could make way for other more sustainable mobility behaviours, by reducing the dependency of most households on their own private means of transport. In fact, many studies consider shared mobility as a promising way to reduce traffic congestion and CO_2 emissions. However, this conclusion needs further evidence, and current literature is not in agreement in this regard. The extent of CO_2 emission reductions largely depends on the type of mobility service. Broadly speaking, only those sharing mobility models that require people not only to share a vehicle, but also to travel together at the same time, are promising in terms of congestion and CO_2 emissions reductions (but they are also the least attractive to individuals in comparison with the privately owned vehicles, given waiting and travel time, comfort and convenience). While the impact of other sharing mobility models that allow customers to use an entire vehicle for a given period of time is dubious, they do not seem to have the potential to reduce congestion or CO_2 emissions substantially.

If we look at sharing mobility from a policy perspective, these practices also seem to be characterised by their 'hybridity'. According to García Canclini, the concept of "*hybridity* has been used by authors in the social sciences, literary, artistic and cultural studies to designate processes in which discrete social practices or structures, that existed in separate ways, combine to generate new structures, objects and practices in which the preceding elements mix"[3]. In our view, the outcome of a hybridisation process can be described as the effect of an intentional—and to some extent creative—exploitation of different existing factors that, after their combination, provide a new system or product made available to society.

Here, hybridity in sharing mobility may be defined as a combination process affecting two different types of resources: firstly, those material elements that enable transport and dwellers to move in space, infrastructure like roads or parking areas, or vehicles such as cars or bikes; secondly, those organisational resources, facilitated by disrupting innovation in the ICT sector, which allow people to access shared assets through the web and to interact within a virtual environment that offers travellers a variety of mobility options. In this perspective, sharing mobility can be read as creative use of traditional elements of the functions of cities—without which services could not work—driven by new cultural values and societal challenges, such as sustainability and collaboration.

The other main reason to consider sharing mobility as an expression of 'hybridity' relates to its economic and political basis. Cohen and Shaheen[4] provide an interesting explanation by distinguishing three different ways sharing mobility should be seen under the lens of public policy: firstly, as a 'social and environmental benefit'; secondly, as a 'sustainable business' and finally, and more explicitly, as a 'business'.

The social and environmental aims of sharing mobility dominate when local government recognises its own role in mitigating various collective costs associated with personal automobile use, including congestion, the inefficiency of public transport, and pollution. In this framework, sharing mobility costs are covered by public authorities; revenues from subscribers are used to co-finance service maintenance, with the remaining costs (virtually) balanced by the benefits received by the local community.

Instead, we can refer to sharing mobility as a 'sustainable business' when services receive a moderate public support. Under this model, local government considers "shared mobility as comprising services that yield social and environmental benefits but are simultaneously revenue-generating enterprises" (Cohen and Shaheen 2018). In this case, municipalities usually provide limited economic support and facilities, while operators are required to cover the remaining costs to maintain the service in operation.

In the last model, shared mobility is seen as a purely business-oriented activity. Local government generally provides little support, which mostly consists of granting/issuing anything that is needed to service implementation (i.e. permits, licences, public rights allocation, etc.), while (private) operators are required to cover the full costs of operations in exchange for profit. Consequently, in contrast to previous models, there is limited (or even no) room to guarantee the public interest, such as pricing policies or agreed standards of service.

In most cases, these three models do not operate separately in urban areas. Public sharing mobility services led by municipalities are often complemented by one or more other services run by private companies. This fact has two major implications on local government and on the way the collective interest is—or has to be—treated by public policy. Firstly, sharing mobility cannot be uniquely referred to the public or the market, but rather, it is seen as an expression of a wide range of stakeholders with different rationales, which can include local authorities, citizens, public and private transport operators, community organisations, NGOs, the media, etc. Secondly, such heterogeneity implies a rigorous multi-stakeholder approach in order to avoid conflicts and inefficiency: public authorities have a key role in taking the decisions on the planning and implementation of services; they need to work closely with the private sector to address issues such as regulation, insurance, business models and equity in order to fully realise the benefits of sharing mobility for the community (CIVITAS 2016).

To work effectively in that complex arena, sharing mobility needs to be pushed over the siloed approaches that often dominate public policy and, we might say, translate into a 'hybridisation' of conventional tools in the hands of local government. One key to turn such hybridity into strength is embedding the sharing mobility concept within the many existing instruments falling within the urban planning domain, such as land use and transportation plans, urban regeneration schemes or climate action plans. Another crucial aspect is investment by cities in civic participation, focusing on sharing mobility at the community/neighbourhood level and going beyond the obvious target of avoiding stakeholder conflicts.

In his chapter, Guido Smorto focuses on several legal issues related to the rise of sharing mobility. In the first part, he outlines the most fundamental transformations that make the case for regulating sharing mobility services quite different from that of conventional transport: the rise of digital intermediaries that provide a 'bilateral market' between two (or more) interdependent groups of economic agents for the provision of mobility services; and the unprecedented chance offered by these digital platforms to professional as well as non-professional drivers to easily access the market for transport services, with the resulting massive provision of transport services by a 'crowd' of individuals. By also reflecting on the effects of the decision of the European Court of Justice in the Uber case, the chapter focuses on how the rise of sharing mobility challenges the current legal framework under EU law. It also identifies those emerging legal issues stemming from the advent of these innovative services, in order to categorise the competing claims that regulators should be considering.

With regard to this, the article not only elaborates on the main concerns related to market regulation, but it also scrutinises those aspects of the sharing mobility that go beyond market and efficiency concerns, to consider those features that are more significant for fostering an inclusive and sustainable society, also discussing whether and how outsourcing these services to profit-oriented digital platforms and private entities may hamper or threaten social inclusion. Moreover, sharing mobility is not only challenging traditional legal categories and old rules, it is also altering the role of different actors involved in regulation and enforcement, generating a significant mismatch between those who are affected by the ongoing changes and the distribution of regulatory responsibilities. As a general rule, principles governing freedom to provide mobility services must be pursued by implementing a common transport policy in accordance with the FEU Treaty. At the same time, being an intrinsically urban phenomenon, sharing mobility affects the traditional organisation of local services, putting into question how urban transportation is planned and redesigning city spaces. In this vein, in its last part the chapter ponders on whether a new regulatory framework is desirable in the light of the ongoing changes, and on the first principles on which such a regulatory framework should rest. Sharing mobility has the potential to change the way we move in a more efficient, sustainable and inclusive way, compared to the alternative modes of transport based on private vehicles. However, a well-targeted, future-proof regulatory framework must be laid down for seizing these opportunities.

In the second chapter, Ignazio Vinci discusses the role sharing mobility services may have in the future organisation of cities and the extent to which they can be treated as a policy tool by local government. Here, cities are seen as a result of the continuous interaction among urban and transport development under the influence of changes in economy and society. For that reason, in the second paragraph the author explores the ways urban development has been shaped by mobility throughout modern history, from the industrial revolution to contemporary cities, when new societal challenges and planning paradigms are emerging. In this context, the third paragraph describes sharing mobility both as an expression of relevant changes in citizens' culture and as a result of disruptive innovation processes in technology. In fact, on the one hand, shared mobility appears to be a response to people's growing sensibility towards the environment and a result of the less importance given—especially by younger generations—to car ownership. On the other hand, the spreading of shared mobility in modern cities must be strictly related to its easy access from smartphones and the web, and to the advantage for users given by the availability of unlimited spatial information, partially shared by the same travellers.

These last features in particular make sharing mobility substantially different from any other conventional form of transport in urban areas. In fact, by giving users a variety of 'context-specific' transport options, sharing mobility allows travellers to establish an extremely flexible relationship with space, with the transit networks and, in turn, with urban places. In other words, through the users/service interaction, these services provide a new spatial order to urban transport, a virtual environment described as a 'mobility ecosystem', characterised by adaptivity and the increased autonomy of travellers. These reasons for success, however, do not remove some of the concerns around the use of sharing mobility within public policy that are critically discussed in the last section of the chapter. For instance, as shared mobility services are an expression of a range of stakeholders with different rationalities—often private operators responding to the market—evidence suggest that these services are unable to address the typical aims of public transport (i.e. the reduction in geographical marginality) and services can be hardly coordinated to other urban policies. Drawing from good practices developed across the world, in the final section the author focuses on certain planning methods and criteria that help to overcome the problems of implementing sharing mobility, increasing its role in the promotion of sustainable development in cities.

In the chapter written by Cristian Inguglia, Martina Di Marco and Miriam Ricci, the authors discuss the connection between social inclusion and urban mobility, exploring the role sharing mobility may have in reducing social marginality. The paper focuses particularly on certain disadvantaged groups such as migrants, who experience well-known difficulties in accessing public transport in urban areas and, even more, in becoming owners of a private vehicle. In this context, sharing mobility is still not seen as a useful transport option to migrants, due to a series of obstacles that include the perception of being 'niche services' targeted at privileged people, economic obstacles deriving from high fees and lack of credit cards and the digital gap associated with the smartphone needed to access the services.

The work starts from the assumption that while the associations between migrants' social inclusion and mobility have already been examined in literature, the potential role sharing mobility could play in this process has not yet been widely analysed. To bridge that gap, after an analysis of the theoretical framework on the mobility–marginality nexus, the authors provide a critical interpretation of the key findings of a focus group study involving residents and migrants in the city of Palermo, Italy. After the introduction, the chapter is structured into two main sections. In the first of these sections, the authors provide a theoretical framework on the relationships between mobility and social exclusion. Here, mobility is described as a crucial element for accessing services and life opportunities and therefore as a key driver for overcoming social exclusion. The reasons for social marginality are explained under the lens of useful concepts found in literature, for instance that of 'transport disadvantage', or the phenomenon of 'transport-related social exclusion' proposed by Lucas (2012). For migrants, it is recognised by the authors, the risks of exclusion are increased by further constraints to accessing transport because of language issues, difficulties in wayfinding and the lack of economic resources.

In the last section and the conclusion, the results of the focus group held with migrants in Palermo are discussed, looking at the development, in the future, of more inclusive sharing mobility services. Interaction with migrants resulted in interesting proposals to remove the obstacles to making sharing mobility an effective policy tool to tackle social marginality. These proposals include the request to adapt the services fees according to users' incomes, to enhance sharing mobility systems also in the outskirts of city and the introduction of integrated subscriptions to incentivise the users of sharing mobility also to utilise public transport.

Starting from a case study held in the Lisbon Metropolitan Area, Joana Vicente, Catarina Rolim and Patrícia Baptista provide an analysis on the potential attractivity to consumers of shared, electric and autonomous mobility. Over the last few years, Portugal's motorisation rate has increased significantly, with the result of creating problems such as traffic congestion and pressure for parking, especially in the main urban areas. This process is also producing a growing environmental impact, considering that transport activities are responsible for around 28% of greenhouse gas emissions in Portugal.

The study started with the assumption that, despite the growing popularity of sharing mobility and electric cars, the spreading of autonomous vehicles is still limited due to different barriers, including purchasing costs and the low security perceived by potential users. Therefore, the authors investigate the acceptability of these types of vehicles to users according to two variables—travel costs and time—and three different alternatives: the first, consisting of the use of a conventional private vehicle, the other two with an autonomous electric vehicle in car-sharing and ride-sharing solutions, respectively. The collected data show on average an acceptance of 44% among respondents, a share that is obtained and affected by some of the variables considered in the analysis. For instance, younger people seem to be more inclined to adopt innovative ways of transport, as people aged below 35 present more than 50% choice in shared, electric and autonomous vehicles. On the contrary, independently of age, people that used to travel outside of the rush-hour period have shown more reluctance to change. Furthermore, choice appears to be affected by previous experiences with the sharing mobility means available in the area, with the respondents who were not willing to try such services showing a clear preference for continuing to use the current alternatives.

Overall, the analysis suggests that a wider adoption of innovative mobility solutions can be achieved if new approaches are to be taken in policy-making. First, there is a need to disseminate the positive impacts of these alternatives, making them easier to use and more accessible to everybody. Second, it is crucial for understanding the reasons why people choose them and therefore, the lifestyles and travel behaviours of potential users. Not least, public policy should help society to embrace the change, making people see mobility as a service rather than as a product, and to consider innovative transport not only as matter of improving city's environment.

In the book's final chapter, Massimo Ciuffini, Luca Refrigeri and Sofia Asperti give an account on the spread of sharing mobility in Italy, a country with the third-highest motorisation rate in the EU, and which in modern history has often neglected the importance of public transport in urban areas. Despite that, the chapter highlights a significant growth of shared mobility in Italian cities, from both the demand and supply side of services.

The first, extensive, section of the paper describes the new paradigms behind the emergence of sharing mobility in contemporary society, as well as the mechanisms and tools that characterise various services made available in urban areas. The paper especially focuses on the interplay between the technological and organisational innovations that enabled such services to shift from a market niche to a popular phenomenon. For instance, the paper emphasises the implications deriving from the adoption of the 'mobility as a service' concept to mobility practices, enabling ICT platforms to provide a variety of integrated transport options, in order to satisfy users' needs with extreme flexibility.

In the second section of the paper, the authors provide an insight into the state of the art of sharing mobility in Italy, both in quantitative and qualitative terms. In recent years, the country has been experiencing significant growth in the number of sharing mobility users, with trips increasing by 26% between 2017 and 2018, up to a total number of 33 million. Also, the number of subscribers increased to 5.2 million in 2018, distributed between different services that in total have reached the number of 363 at national level. Around one-third of subscribers (1.8 million) are car-sharing users, 90% of whom concentrate on free-floating services. Innovation processes also include the spread of electric and light vehicles—increasing from 27 to 43% between 2017 and 2018—and the boom of digital platforms with functions of 'mobility aggregators' among public transport and shared mobility operators. Overall, in 2018, the Italian cities served by shared mobility services amounted to 34.

In the concluding remarks, the authors suggest a series of political and technical issues that should be removed to limit the primacy of individual mobility to the advantage of shared mobility. These include a series of legal barriers that are still impeding market entry to some innovative shared mobility services, the need to harmonise the regulatory framework in the whole country and, accordingly, the quest for more effective coordination among transport policies at local level.

Against this backdrop, the main focus of the book is the intersection between sharing mobility and the urban environment, exploring the links between sharing mobility and urban policy understood as a complex system of government and planning activities with the contribution of different actors and stakeholders. In such a fast-evolving urban transport environment, striking a balance between market uniformity and city experimentation is perhaps the most significant challenge for a European common policy in the transport sector in the years ahead.

Notes

1 The terms "sharing mobility" and "shared mobility" are both widely employed in current literature, and they are used interchangeably in this book.
2 Jean Monnet Project "*Regulating and Deregulating Sharing Mobility in Europe*". Erasmus + Programme Jean Monnet Activities 2018—Call for Proposals EAC/A05/2017—Ref. 599384-EPP-1–2018-1-IT-EPPJMO-PROJECT (Scientific Coordinator Guido Smorto).
3 García Canclini (2001).
4 Cohen and Shaheen (2018).

References

Cohen, A., & Shaheen, S. (2018). *Planning for shared mobility*. Chicago: American Planning Association.

Civitas. (2016). Smart choices for cities. *Cities towards mobility 2.0: Connect, share and go!* Brussels: Civitas Consortium.

García Canclini, N. (2001). Hybridity. In *International encyclopedia of the social & behavioral sciences*. Elsevier

Lucas, K. (2012). Transport and social exclusion: Where are we now?. *Transport Policy, 20*, 105–113. https://doi.org/10.1016/j.tranpol.2012.01.013.

Regulating and Deregulating Sharing Mobility in Europe

Guido Smorto

Abstract This chapter gives an account of the many legal issues related to the rise of sharing mobility in Europe, as part of the activities carried out within the 2018–2020 Jean Monnet Project "*Regulating and Deregulating Sharing Mobility in Europe*" (RIDER). In the first part, it outlines the most fundamental economic transformations that make the case for regulating sharing mobility services quite different from conventional transport. By also referring to the activities carried out during the project, it identifies those emerging legal issues stemming from the advent of sharing mobility, in order to categorize the competing claims that regulators should be considering when facing these innovative practices. With regard to this, the article outlines the main concerns related to market regulation, and it illustrates those aspects of the sharing mobility that go beyond market and efficiency concerns, to consider those features that are more significant for fostering an inclusive and sustainable society. As RIDER clearly demonstrated, sharing mobility has the potential to change the way we move in a more efficient, sustainable and inclusive way. However, a well-targeted, future-proof regulatory framework must be laid down for seizing these opportunities.

Keywords Sharing economy · Sharing mobility · Online digital intermediaries · Peer-to-peer economy · EU law

1 The Quest for a Common Transport Policy in Europe

Mobility has always been understood as one of the main common policy areas of the European Economic Community and a cornerstone of European integration since the Treaty of Rome.[1] Nonetheless, Member States have always been reluctant to relinquish sovereignty over their transport infrastructure and to give up national legislation in favor of a common European framework of rules.[2] The European Parliament has even brought the EU Council before the European Court of Justice for this lack of a

G. Smorto (✉)
Department of Law, University of Palermo, Palermo, Italy
e-mail: guido.smorto@unipa.it

G. Smorto and I. Vinci (eds.), *The Role of Sharing Mobility in Contemporary Cities*, UNIPA Springer Series, https://doi.org/10.1007/978-3-030-57725-4_2

common transport policy. After a historical decision recognizing that the Council had failed to ensure freedom to provide services in the field of transport,[3] a White Paper was issued by the Commission which mentions transport as central for fostering the internal market.[4] Even then, European institutions did not exercise their competence to implement a common transport policy, with the only legislative initiatives taken on mobility at European level mostly based on environmental concerns and/or to guarantee passengers' rights.[5] As the 2011 EC White Paper on Transport denounced, a lot still needs to be done to complete the internal market for transport in Europe: a verdict that may still be considered valid today.[6]

There are many potential drawbacks to the lack of a common policy in such a strategic sector. According to the EU, transport is global and the transport industry accounted for about five percent of European GDP in 2019. A transport policy would be instrumental to the implementation of a Common Market and an essential element for the free movement of persons, services and goods. This absence is even more relevant in face of the digital revolution. Internet, GPS and smartphones have resulted in a radical lowering of communication costs, coordination and monitoring of behaviors, thus promoting the dissemination of innovative models of mobility services, with tech companies for sharing mobility operating throughout the European market, thanks to digital platforms that make use of big data, artificial intelligence and data management in order to provide a reliable and convenient service to their customers across Europe.

As part of the activities carried out within the 2018–2020 Jean Monnet Project "*Regulating and Deregulating Sharing Mobility in Europe*" (RIDER), this article scrutinizes the impact of digital technology in the transport sector, with special regard to sharing mobility services, and the emerging legal issues stemming from the advent of these innovative business models, in order to categorize the competing, and sometimes diverging, features that regulators should be considering. By also referring to the activities carried out during RIDER, the article first describes the main legal issues related to market regulation of sharing mobility (§§ 2–4). Then, it inspects those aspects of the sharing mobility that go beyond market regulation, in order to consider how to foster an inclusive mobility (§ 5). In its last part, it appraises whether a new regulatory framework is desirable in the light of the ongoing changes and it defines the first principles that should inspire new policies and rules for sharing mobility in Europe (§§ 6–7).

2 The Rise of Sharing Mobility

"Sharing mobility" identifies a diverse range of innovative transport services based on temporary access to resources, facilitated by digital intermediaries that provide an open marketplace to mitigate coordination problems between supply and demand, for the conclusion of transactions between decentralized economic agents, either private individuals and professionals, each belonging to one of the sides of the market (e.g., drivers and passengers).[7] Framed this way, sharing mobility is part of the so-called sharing economy—a term commonly used to describe those innovative economic systems that employ digital technologies to enable the exchange of goods and the supply of services by a decentralized "crowd" of individuals (Sundararajan 2016).

Central to this business model is the exploitation of the so-called idling capacity, i.e. the use of distinctive type of resources—typically, renewable ones and those subject to rapid decay—closer to their full capacity.[8] By tapping into this spare capacity, it is possible to deliver innovative services based on the shared use of resources. Cars are the representative cases of renewable resources; seats in a car for a given trip (e.g., a ride from Paris to Brussels on day x) are an illustrative example of resources subject to rapid decay. Correspondingly, carsharing is a way to share almost perfectly renewable resources, like cars; ridesharing is a way to share high decay rate resources, such as seats in a car for a given trip.[9] As these examples make clear, transport is one of the sectors most impacted by digital technologies, with the widespread adoption of an access-based model of consumption of services that is replacing and/or complementing ownership models for mobility. Digital intermediaries, such as Uber, Lyft and BlaBlaCar, are the most prominent cases of such large-scale coordination of supply and demand for providing transport services among individuals. After all, being parked for most of their life cycle and, when used, often occupied only by the driver without passengers, automobiles are possibly the most striking pool of underutilized capital existing in the world (Sundararajan 2016, 115).

3 Regulating Digital Intermediaries for Sharing Mobility Services

As emerged throughout the entire JM Project, appropriate rules for sharing mobility must first consider two fundamental transformations in business models that make the case for regulating sharing mobility services quite different from conventional transport. The first change is the rise of digital intermediaries that provide a "bilateral market" between two (or more) interdependent groups of economic agents for the provision of mobility services.[10] Closely related to this first transformation is the massive-scale provision of transport services by a "crowd" of individuals, whether professionals or "peers" (i.e., non-professionals), who offer their goods and services for mobility to the public via digital platforms that coordinate demand and supply.

Most digital intermediaries for the provision of mobility services describe themselves as "marketplaces": providers of online transactional services for facilitating the exchange of goods and services by independent economic agents.[11] Legally, these digital intermediaries that enable the supply of transport services by a "crowd" of individual providers may be deemed, alternatively, to offer a transport service themselves or to provide a mere digital intermediation between demand and supply by enabling their users to locate, book and pay for a transport service provided by someone else.

Under EU law, this distinction is of the utmost importance. Mere digital intermediation for the exchange of goods and services shall be considered as an "information society service"—a "service normally provided for remuneration, at a distance, by electronic means and at the individual request of a recipient of services"[12]—a key category of EU law, as it gives a wide-ranging freedom and considerable discretion in providing services in the internal market. According to EU law, those who provide information society services are subject to lighter rules, and Member States are restricted in their ability to establish authorization schemes for these activities. Furthermore, in such a case, rules on transport can only be enforced against individual users of the platform, who are the only ones responsible for ensuring a safe and reliable service. At the opposite end of the scale, if deemed as offering transport services themselves, platforms are subject to sector-specific rules and market access requirements for the "underlying service," including business authorization and licensing requirements.

Another primary point that surfaced in the discussion during RIDER is that this critical distinction between "information society service" and the "underlying service" is even more relevant when the "underlying service" is transport. The transport sector falls under Title VI of the TFEU, and it does not benefit from the free movement provisions of the TFEU and the "Services Directive".[13] As a consequence, not only is the lighter, uniform regime for "information society services" ruled out, but also, the general freedom to provide services under the Service Directive. In contrast, those who provide transport services are subject to sector-specific regulations and required to comply with each national, regional and local law (which are extremely variable on a local basis) in order to obtain the necessary licenses and authorizations requested in almost all European countries. Given the flexible nature of business models adopted by digital platforms for sharing mobility services, well-defined principles are needed for a case-by-case appraisal of their nature. After the European Commission first tackled the issue in its Communication on "A European agenda for the collaborative economy",[14] the question has been addressed by the European Court of Justice in *Uber Spain*[15] and *Uber France*.[16] The Spanish case originated in 2015, when the Commercial Court No. 3 of Barcelona sent a request for a preliminary ruling to the CJEU regarding the extent to which Uber Systems Spain, S.L.—which operated its services in Barcelona, Madrid and Valencia, without authorization from the Spanish authorities[17]—should benefit from the free movement provisions contained in the Services Directive and/or the e-Commerce Directive, as well as in the provisions of the TFEU. The core legal question raised by the referring Court under EU law was whether the "peer-to-peer" ridesharing service offered by UberPop should be considered as an "information society service" or as transport. The European Court of Justice finally ruled that "an intermediation service, the purpose of which is to connect, by means of a smartphone application and for remuneration, non-professional drivers using their own vehicle with persons who wish to make urban journeys, *must be regarded as being inherently linked to a transport service and, accordingly, must be classified as 'a service in the field of transport'* within the meaning of EU law, and it must be excluded from the scope of the freedom to provide services in general as well as the directive on services in the internal market and the directive on electronic commerce" (emphasis added).[18] In reaching the decision, the Court followed its own precedents, according to which the concept of "services in the field of transport" includes not only transport services per se, but also any service inherently linked to any physical act of moving persons or goods from one place to another by means of transport.[19] In principle, a service "consisting of connecting a non-professional driver using his or her own vehicle with a person who wishes to make an urban journey" is a separate service from a transport service and meets the criteria for classification as an "information society service" (§§ 34–35). But only a "mere intermediation" among truly independent economic agents, without any significant control exerted by the platform over the substantive service offered by its users, enjoys the status of "information society service." On the contrary, Uber provides a "composite service," where the intermediation forms an integral part of an overall service whose main component is a transport service, as it exercises a "decisive control" over the essential procedures for the provision of the underlying service, and it created "a new supply that did not exist before".[20] Accordingly, it must be classified as "a service in the field of transport," not as "an information society service" (§ 40).[21]

4 Regulating Crowd-Based Mobility Services

The other key legal issue investigated during RIDER is the unprecedented chance offered by digital platforms to professional and non-professional drivers to easily access the market for transport services. This transformation poses another considerable challenge to the existing legal framework, as it puts into question the applicability of professional rules to individual service providers. Since the line, once very clear, between professionals and non-professionals is more and more confused, it is increasingly difficult to define distinctive rules for the two categories, and a case-by-case assessment is needed.[22]

All over Europe, the transport sector has always been especially strict in this regard, with the supply of transport services firmly reserved to professional providers. Member States routinely require an administrative permission or authorization in order to operate as a driver for the transport of passengers. Conditions for obtaining professional licenses differ greatly across countries, but in general they are issued based on qualitative[23] and sometimes quantitative[24] requirements, and frequent geographical restrictions, with the most common justifications referring to public security, public order, safety and minimum service obligations as grounds for restricting the free provision of services.

As a general rule, the European hire transport market is subdivided into two main segments: (i) hailing and ranking; and (ii) pre-booked. The majority of Member States adopt this two-tier system, with private hire vehicles (PHVs) and similar services organized around a different set of rules than taxis.[25] Generally speaking, taxis and PHVs can operate in the pre-booked segment, while taxi services enjoy a legal monopoly on the hail segment. Typically, PHVs are under an obligation to perform the service based on a prior reservation and to return to the garage or to the place of business after each ride, unless a new request for transportation has been received. Correspondingly, while both these activities are reserved to professional drivers under authorizations, conditions to provide PHVs are usually less stringent than those applicable to taxis.[26]

Against this legal framework, even before *Uber Spain*, many Member States had undertaken regulatory initiatives in response to the rise of sharing mobility services. A few Member States had opened up to "occasional services" rendered by non-professionals, allowing peer-to-peer transport services intermediated by online platforms and making non-professional drivers subject to a lighter regime compared to taxis.[27] However, in most cases, a strong regulatory backlash had taken place all over Europe, with the overall majority of Member States maintaining the ban for non-professional drivers to operate as providers of mobility services via digital platforms and prohibiting or severely constraining peer-to-peer ridesharing services almost everywhere in Europe. This holds true for France,[28] Spain,[29] Belgium,[30] the Netherlands,[31] Germany,[32] Italy[33] and the UK, among others.[34] With regard to this, *Uber Spain* confirmed an existing trend, affirming that the use of digital platforms does not rule out the need for transportation licenses (or equivalent authorizations) for drivers, in compliance with local transport regulation. In commenting on the decision, Uber itself declared that *Uber Spain* would have had a limited impact on its business.[35]

5 Beyond Market Regulation. An Inclusive Sharing Mobility

Thanks to the interdisciplinary nature of the team, RIDER was also able to focus on aspects of sharing mobility other than market regulation. Indeed, the case for regulating sharing mobility is not just a matter of appropriate rules both for digital intermediaries and individual service providers.[36] Its distributive impact is also crucial for sound regulation. Since mobility is vital to people's lives, and lack of transport services may hamper opportunities, determine social exclusion and cause economic hardship, it is extremely important to assess how sharing mobility services impact different segments of population and individuals, in order to promote an inclusive mobility and to address potential inequalities in service delivery. Truly inclusive transport services must be affordable and accessible to anyone, and they should benefit all individuals and groups, even marginalized ones that do not have financial means and/or digital literacy to enjoy new services.

This has led to thoughts on how outsourcing these services to profit-oriented digital platforms and private entities may hamper or threaten social inclusion. In principle, by connecting people to share assets, services or both, sharing mobility may facilitate a more efficient use of under-utilized resources, becoming a powerful tool of economic growth and social inclusion. However, the economic and social impact of sharing mobility have not been adequately explored enough, and, so far, evidence is conflicting (Ranchordas 2020). Some studies testify how ridesharing services are mainly used by mid-/high income users, it being too expensive compared to public transportation (McKinsey Global Institute 2018). Other studies point to a different direction and conclude that sharing mobility services potentially benefit the below-median-income part of the population more than the above-median-income one and that sharing firms can be used as means to redistribute income (Fraiberger and Sundararajan 2015; Dillahunt and Malone 2015).

In this regard, denial of market access to disadvantaged individuals or groups is a rising concern when comparing innovative sharing services with traditional ones. Taxis are typically required to serve poor areas of the city, to have cars equipped to accommodate customers with disabilities and to apply the same rate based on distance regardless of the area. On the contrary, digital platforms offering mobility as a service are not subject to the same constraints, and they are largely responsive only to market forces. They may accept rides based on their profitability, they are not under a duty to take expensive steps to accommodate customers, and they may limit their operation area to the city center, leaving the unprofitable suburbs and loss-making services to traditional public services. Given the role that sharing mobility can play in this regard, sharing mobility services should be open to vulnerable groups, such as low-income and/or low-educated people, minorities, migrants, elderly people and so on. Furthermore, digital skills and digital literacy are pivotal to have access to these services, and it is crucial to avoid the risk of creating a potential technological hurdle that may impede or deter access to a significant part of the population.

6 First Principles for Regulating Sharing Mobility in Europe

Following the discussion made throughout RIDER, first principles for a common transport policy for sharing mobility services have been identified. Strong support has been expressed on the suitability of equal treatment of traditional and digital companies whenever they provide comparable transport services, regardless of the way these services are delivered, whether in conventional or innovative ways. This is deemed to be especially critical in the transport sector, as it would help to overcome the current all-or-nothing approach that the distinction between "information society services" and "services in the field of transport" entails, in accordance with Title VI of the TFEU, the Services Directive, and the e-Commerce Directive (see *supra*, par. 3), with the risk of regulatory arbitrage between digital and traditional companies providing similar services. When digital platforms employ an innovative way to offer a transport service akin to those offered by traditional companies, they should be subject to the same regulation as conventional offline providers, and the same rules should apply to digital as well as traditional companies that offer the same real-world service in different ways. As the Advocate General puts it in *Uber Spain*, "indirect control such as that exercised by Uber, based on financial incentives and decentralized passenger-led ratings, with a scale effect, makes it possible to manage in a way that is just as—if not more—effective than management based on formal orders given by an employer to his employees and direct control over the carrying out of such orders" (para. 52). Thus, it would be artificial to distinguish between a service that is provided by electronic means and one that is not, where the two supplies are so closely linked to each other and are provided by the same economic actor.[37] And any different treatment for intermediation platforms that provide an equivalent service to the one offered by traditional companies amounts to regulatory arbitrage to be prevented.

Along the same lines, the importance of avoiding regulatory arbitrage between similarly situated individual service providers has also been expressed over the course of RIDER, given that the *Uber* case outlawed peer-to-peer mobility services. Since public safety and quality of service are the main conventional justifications for regulatory intervention, a far-reaching reconsideration of rules for professionals should be made, reviewing existing national legislation and simplifying procedures and formalities for service providers, in order to avoid unfair competition among analogous categories of economic agents.

As an example, market separation between taxi and other hire transport services is increasingly difficult to justify, especially in the pre-booked market.[38] This market segment has recently fostered fierce competition among various intermediaries, with price competition and new technologies that have eroded the taxi market share. Restrictions may still be justified in street hail, as this segment may actually display special safety needs, since the driver and the rider do not know each other, so that information asymmetries may occur. However, most rules for the pre-booked market are no longer justified to accomplish public interests, and they run the risk of shielding license holders against competition from new entrants without any sound justification. Even those disadvantages that taxis may suffer from being subject to fixed prices and obligation to contract with any passenger are negligible in a competitive market. Moreover, the traditional separation between taxis and PHVs in the pre-booked market is not only hard to justify in the light of technological evolution, but it may be detrimental for an efficient and sustainable provision of the service (Dempsey 1996). In 2020, the Italian Constitutional Court held that the obligation upon PHVs to return to the garage or to the place of business after each ride entails an unreasonable organizational and administrative burden, finding it unconstitutional. As the Court affirms, such an obligation is disproportionate to the objective of ensuring that the PHV service is not aimed at the general public, and the need to return to the garage to collect the requests of new services can be overcome, without interfering with the taxi service, thanks to technological tools and appropriate rules for technological platforms that intermediate supply and demand for mobility services.[39]

The removal of the obligation to return empty after a ride outside the area of authorization and the elimination of the return to garage rule for hire cars with driver may be beneficial, as these measures would help to diminish congestion and to reduce prices since passengers would not have to pay for a trip fare where it is requested (Frazzani et al. 2016, 159). Moreover, the use of new technologies has consistently reduced waiting times, so that competition in the pre-booked segment has also affected the hailing and rank segment.[40] Given this background, it is hardly surprising that many competition authorities all over Europe advocate for a more competitive transport market.[41]

Finally, as widely discussed in the RIDER events devoted to social inclusion, a regulatory framework for an inclusive sharing mobility is especially desirable to prevent a disparate impact on different segments of the population and to avoid discrimination and unequal access to transport services. In order to grant effective, equal access to transportation to the benefit of those who do not have financial means, have a limited ability to travel and/or lack digital skills to use these services, sharing mobility platforms must be put under public obligation to accommodate every customer. Sharing mobility services must serve those areas that are underserved by public transport, and public authorities should hold these companies responsible for failing to take reasonable steps to make these services available to poor urban residents, migrants, people with disabilities or underserved communities. Public authorities should be able to mandate these companies to operate in poor and underserved areas and to accommodate low-income or minority communities and people with disabilities, to prescribe specific requirements to meet these needs (e.g., equipping at least part of the fleet of vehicles with ramps for people requiring special assistance), or to establish a funding pool for these purposes.

7 Conclusive Remarks. Regulatory Responsibilities for Sharing Mobility in Europe

As emerged during RIDER, sharing mobility is not only challenging traditional legal categories and old rules, but it is also altering the role of different actors involved in regulation and enforcement, generating a significant mismatch between those who are affected by the ongoing changes and the distribution of regulatory responsibilities.

During the many events held within the Project, there was broad consensus that uniform rules across Europe are needed in order to avoid a fragmented market for transport services. As the same EU Commission emphasized in its 2011 White Paper, the only way to address global challenges is to enhance convergence of rules.[42] In the last part of *Uber Spain*, the Court underlines that, being classified as "a service in the field of transport," innovative mobility services are covered by the European common transport policy, so that principles governing freedom to provide services are not ruled out, but they must be pursued by implementing a common transport policy in accordance with the FEU Treaty.[43]

Beside Member States hesitancy, a more ambitious policy framework may have been so far inhibited by the subsidiarity principle, which sets out when the Union should intervene, acting within its powers and thus curbing legal measures adopted by the EU on transport mostly to environmental concerns and/or passengers' rights. Nonetheless, technology may shift this limit, making a local problem a general one which may now be better addressed at European level by reason of its scale and effects.[44]

On the other hand, as another related JM Project has highlighted,[45] sharing mobility affects the traditional organization of local services, putting into question how urban transportation is planned and redesigning city spaces. Hence, sharing mobility is an intrinsically urban phenomenon (Davidson and Infranca 2016). Innovative solutions for mobility may help to solve the urban density and congestion risks which typically afflict urban spaces and at the same time, they may also provoke local scale externalities and intensified use of urban resources and local services. However, while cities are the most affected by these changes, they do not always have adequate tools to deal with them or to regulate them in accordance with their needs (Smorto 2016).

New regulations for sharing mobility also call into question the role and responsibilities of digital platforms. Online intermediaries are often described as actors participating in the regulatory chain, also collaborating with public authorities in monitoring compliance (Busch 2020). However, the ability of public authorities to efficiently regulate offline services intermediated by digital platforms is often impaired by the resistance of digital intermediaries to share data and to enforce public regulation.[46]

This opposition makes public authorities dependent on private firms to provide essential services when data is needed, and public enforcement unnecessarily difficult and costly, as it leaves public authorities with no choice but to enforce regulation toward a distributed and heterogeneous "crowd" of economic agents. On the contrary, being best positioned as intermediaries between supply and demand, platforms should be liable for enforcing substantive regulation and quality standards, regardless of their nature as mere intermediaries or providers of the service, whenever these platforms make their profits from the offline services and are able to enforce regulation in a more cost-effective way than public authorities.

Data are central to this strategy. Sharing mobility services rely on ubiquitous digital devices, with sensors that ascertain and communicate real-time location and predict future position, thanks to GPS and communication networks. The ability of digital intermediaries to collect personal data for tracking and profiling users has not only obvious consequences for the personal privacy of users and customers, but it also raises other fears related to the dominance exercised by platforms in information gathering, as this data is typically not available to public authorities, with private companies usually opposing their property rights on it (whether sui generis rights or trade secrets).[47] However, data held by private companies can be extremely relevant to guide policy decisions or to improve public services. These data can be used to better urban planning, road safety and traffic management, as well as for better environmental protection and consumer protection (EC 2018b). Thus, it is crucial to improve access for public authorities to private-sector data whenever a clear and demonstrable public interest is present (EC 2018a, b). Access to and reuse of private-sector data are central to any strategy for the use of public spaces and infrastructures and to take informed decisions, and public authorities should be able to acquire all potential public interest information from firms, provided that restrictions are needed based on protocols for data use, retention and deletion,[48] with public authorities also sharing their data with private companies, making the exchange mutually beneficial (EC 2020).

As RIDER clearly demonstrated, sharing mobility has the potential to change the way we move in a more efficient, sustainable and inclusive way, compared to the alternative modes of transport based on private vehicles. However, a well-targeted, future-proof regulatory framework must be laid down for seizing these opportunities. This holds true for the content of new rules and, even more, for the distribution of regulatory responsibilities. A European common transport policy is surely desirable to overcome the regulatory standstill that affects sharing mobility services all over Europe and to prevent a strategic sector from being subject to divergent national and local rules. At the same time, it remains essential to leave room for local authorities to generate distinct, context-dependent, strategies and tailored regulatory responses. Striking a balance between market uniformity and city experimentation[49] is the most relevant challenge for a European common policy for the transport sector in the years ahead.

Notes

1 This article and the whole book are part of the activities carried out within the 2018–2020 Jean Monnet Project "*Regulating and Deregulating Sharing Mobility in Europe*" (Scientific Coordinator Guido Smorto). Erasmus + Programme Jean Monnet Activities 2018—Call for Proposals EAC/A05/2017—Ref. 599384-EPP-1–2018-1-IT-EPPJMO-PROJECT. The European Commission support for the production of this publication does not constitute an endorsement of the contents which reflects the views only of the author(s), and the Commission cannot be held responsible for any use which may be made of the information contained therein.

2 Cf. Title IV Rome Treaty ("Transport", art. 74–84) sets out a set of substantive and procedural rules, most of which still stand firm today.

3 Case C-13/83 *Parliament v Council*, ECLI:EU:C:1985:220.

4 EC—European Commission (1985), par. 108 ss. ("The right to provide transport services freely throughout the Community is an important part of the Common Transport Policy set out in the Treaty").

5 Cf. Directive 2008/50/EC of the European Parliament and of the Council of May 21, 2008, on ambient air quality and cleaner air for Europe.
OJ L 152, 11.6.2008. See also Directive (EU) 2015/2302 of the European Parliament and of the Council of November 25, 2015, on package travel and linked travel arrangements, amending Regulation (EC) No. 2006/2004 and Directive 2011/83/EU of the European Parliament and of the Council and repealing Council Directive 90/314/EEC, *OJ L 326*, 11.12.2015; Directive 2011/83/EU of the European Parliament and of the Council of October 25, 2011, on consumer rights, amending Council Directive 93/13/EEC and Directive 1999/44/EC of the European Parliament and of the Council and repealing Council Directive 85/577/EEC and Directive 97/7/EC of the European Parliament and of the Council Text with EEA relevance, OJ L 304, 22.11.2011; Regulation (EC) No.

261/2004 of the European Parliament and of the Council of February 11, 2004, establishing common rules on compensation and assistance to passengers in the event of denied boarding and of cancelation or long delay of flights, and repealing Regulation (EEC) No. 295/91 (Text with EEA relevance—Commission Statement, OJ L 46, 17.2.2004; Council Regulation (EC) No. 2027/97 of October 9, 1997, on air carrier liability in the event of accidents, OJ L 285, 17.10.1997; Regulation (EC) No. 1371/2007 of the European Parliament and of the Council of October 23, 2007, on rail passengers' rights and obligations, OJ L 315, 3.12.2007; Regulation (EU) No. 1177/2010 of the European Parliament and of the Council of November 24, 2010, concerning the rights of passengers when traveling by sea and inland waterway and amending Regulation (EC) No. 2006/2004 Text with EEA relevance, OJ L 334, 17.12.2010; Regulation (EU) No. 181/2011 of the European Parliament and of the Council of February 16, 2011, concerning the rights of passengers in bus and coach transport and amending Regulation (EC) No. 2006/2004 Text with EEA relevance, OJ L 55, 28.2.2011. See also Council Directive 85/374/EEC of July 25, 1985, on the approximation of the laws, regulations and administrative provisions of the Member States concerning liability for defective products, OJ L 210, 7.8.1985; Council Directive 90/314/EEC of June 13, 1990, on package travel, package holidays and package tours, OJ L 158, 23.6.1990; Council Regulation (EEC) No. 295/91 of February 4, 1991, establishing common rules for a denied-boarding compensation system in scheduled air transport, OJ L 36, 8.2.1991; Council Directive 93/13/EEC of April 5, 1993, on unfair terms in consumer contracts, *OJ L 95, 21.4.1993*; Directive 97/7/EC of the European Parliament and of the Council of May 20, 1997, on the protection of consumers in respect of distance contracts—Statement by the Council and the Parliament re Article 6(1)—Statement by the Commission re Article 3(1), first indent, OJ L 144, 4.6.1997; Directive 1999/44/EC of the European Parliament and of the Council of May 25, 1999, on certain aspects of the sale of consumer goods and associated guarantees, OJ L 171, 7.7.1999; Directive 2002/65/EC of the European Parliament and of the Council of September 23, 2002, concerning the distance marketing of consumer financial services and amending Council Directive 90/619/EEC and Directives 97/7/EC and 98/27/EC, OJ L 271, 9.10.2002.

6 Cf. EC—European Commission (2011), para. 4. Cf. Colangelo and Zeno-Zencovich (2019, 4) ("In many aspects the rules set out in the TFEU are very similar to the provisions of the Rome Treaty and tend to reproduce them").

7 Notably, "sharing mobility" is also employed to label those access-based, temporary consumption models based on the direct provision of transport services by a company to its customers. The conventional example here is carsharing operated by business entities that provide their services to customers by renting out their own goods. Despite common terminology, these two business models are very different; whereas, a significant legal uncertainty accompanied the spread of digital, crowd-based intermediaries for transport services, the same does not hold true for companies that provide direct access to their goods by temporarily

renting them out. For this reason, in this article, we refer only to digital platforms that intermediate the provision of mobility services.

8 The first group designates those resources that provide a given functionality in any moment of their existence, regardless of whether they have been used previously and whose life cycle is relatively independent from their actual use; the second one defines those resources that, once put into use, produce an excess capacity that can be exploited only within a limited time frame. See Benkler (2004).

9 As the demand for functionality changes from user to user—the use of a car use by the owners is highly variable—and since these assets have a fixed capacity, it is easy to assume that not all buyers are able to use up the full functionality (and cars spend most of their life cycle parked). When the consumption of a given good by its purchaser is lower than the block of functionality sold, this good is under-utilized. However, this unexploited capacity can be given away to third parties by sharing the resource. Moreover, giving away the un-utilized capacity is deemed to be rational whenever it is possible to get any economic or social utility from this giving. Allowing access to a shareable good does not involve any cost for the owner, different from those related to the giving. On the contrary, the cost of exclusion is mainly linked to the so-called opportunity cost, i.e., the absence of an economic or other kind of utility potentially deriving from the inclusion of others. There are cases, however, where the cost of allowing access to third parties is higher than that associated with total exclusion, as when there is a high risk of congestion. When the cost of (selectively or not) including the others is higher total exclusion, then the exclusion is the most efficient choice. Cf. Benkler (2004, 305 ss).

10 On *two-sided markets,* see Rochet and Tirole (2003), Evans and Schmalensee (2007), Rysman (2009), Caillaud and Jullien (2003) and Evans (2003).

11 Cfr. Uber Guidelines for Law Enforcement Authorities: "Uber is a technology company that has developed an app that connects users (riders) with driver partners who provide transportation to the user." https://www.uber.com/it/legal/data-requests/guidelines-for-law-enforcement/en/. Even when platforms provide tools to reduce risks and offer guarantees (insurance, security deposits, alternative dispute resolution mechanisms) such remedies are always presented as voluntary, with no formal assumption of legal obligations. Cf. also Uber Terms of Use § 2. *The Service* ("The Services constitute a technology platform that enables users of Uber's mobile applications or websites provided as part of the Services (each, an 'Application') to arrange and schedule transportation and/or logistics services with independent third party providers of such services (…) You acknowledge that Uber does not provide transportation"), https://www.uber.com/legal/terms/be-en/.

12 "Information society service" is "any service normally provided for remuneration, at a distance, by electronic means and at the individual request of a recipient of services" (art. 1(2) Directive 98/34/EC). See also Article 1(2) of the Directive 98/48/EC of the European Parliament and of the Council of July 20, 1998,

amending Directive 98/34/EC laying down a procedure for the provision of information in the field of technical standards and regulations OJ L 217, 5.8.1998, 18; Article 1(1)(b) of the revised Directive (EU) 2015/1535 of the European Parliament and of the Council of September 9, 2015, laying down a procedure for the provision of information in the field of technical regulations and of rules on Information Society services (Text with EEA relevance) OJ L 241, 17.9.2015, 1. See also Article 3(2) and Articles 12–15 of the Directive 2000/31/EC of the European Parliament and of the Council of June 8, 2000, on certain legal aspects of information society services, in particular electronic commerce, in the Internal Market ("Directive on electronic commerce") OJ L 178, 17.7.2000, 1 (ECD). Cf. C-324/09 Judgment of the Court (Grand Chamber) of July 12, 2011, *L'Oréal SA and Others v eBay International AG and Others*, 2011 ECR I-06011, par. 109 ("an internet service consisting in facilitating relations between sellers and buyers of goods is, in principle, a service for the purposes of Directive 2000/31 (…) It is apparent from the definition of 'information society service', cited at paragraphs 8 and 9 of this judgment, that that concept encompasses services provided at a distance by means of electronic equipment for the processing and storage of data, at the individual request of a recipient of services and, normally, for remuneration. It is clear that the operation of an online marketplace can bring all those elements into play"); and par. 123 ("Article 14(1) of Directive 2000/31 must be interpreted as applying to the operator of an online marketplace where that operator has not played an active role allowing it to have knowledge or control of the data stored").

13 Cf. Articles 56 and 58(1) TFEU, and Article 2(2)(d) Directive 2006/123/EC of the European Parliament and of the Council of December 12, 2006, on services in the internal market, OJ L 376, 27.12.2006.

14 EC—European Commission (2016). The Communication focuses on the degree of control exercised by the platform on the provision of the underlying service, in order to determine the law applicable to digital intermediaries: the platform's responsibility must be assessed with greater rigor when it exercises a strict control on the transaction and on information and communication, it lays down the rules of the exchange, exercise a rigorous supervision, and it influences or even decides the price for the service. Along these lines, the Commission lays down several factual and legal criteria that can play a role in this ad hoc assessment, based on whether the collaborative platform: (a) set or recommend the final price to be paid; (b) set key contractual terms, other than price; (c) own the key assets used to provide the underlying service. In addition, other relevant factors are also mentioned by the Communication, based on whether: The collaborative platform incurs the costs and assumes all the risks related to the provision of the underlying service; an employment relationship exists between the collaborative platform and the person providing the underlying service. When most criteria are met, there are strong indications that the collaborative platform exercises a significant influence or control over the provider of the underlying service, thus acting as a service provider employing peers to perform the offered

services. While the contrary is true when a small degree of influence and control is exerted.

15 C-435/15 *Asociación Profesional Élite Taxi v Uber Systems Spain SL*, ECLI:EU:C:2017:981, Judgment of December 20, 2017, par. 48; C-320/16 *Uber France SAS*, ECLI:C:2018:221, Judgment of April 10, 2018.

16 C-320/16 *Uber France SAS*. Uber's "Pop" service was taken to court by a taxi driver in Lille, who argued the company was breaking the law. The formal issue is regarded whether it constitutes a technical regulation concerning an information society service within the meaning of Directive 98/34 on technical standards and regulations. As the French authorities had not notified the draft law to the Commission before its promulgation, Uber France considered that it could not be prosecuted on the charges set out above. The ECJ concluded that UberPop is a transport service, so that rules about illegal exercise of transport activity are not "technical regulation," and their notification to the Commission is not necessary. That directive requires Member States to notify the Commission of any draft law or rules laying down technical regulations relating to products and information society services. According to the Court, UberPop does not constitute an information society service, and Directive 98/34 is thus not applicable and notifies the draft law to the Commission was unnecessary.

17 Cf. Article 99(1) Law 16/1987 on the organization of land transport, local Regulation on taxi services in Barcelona.

18 C-435/15 *Asociación Profesional Élite Taxi v Uber Systems Spain SL.*

19 See C-168/14, judgment of October 15, 2015, *Grupo Itevelesa and Others*, EU:C:2015:685, paragraphs 45 and 46, and Opinion 2/15 (*Free Trade Agreement with Singapore*) of May 16, 2017, EU:C:2017:376, par. 61. Services that enjoy the substantial freedom contemplated by the e-Commerce Directive are those which take place entirely online. Cf. also "Directive on electronic commerce," Recital 18.

20 In *Uber Spain,* the European Court of Justice adopts a three-step test. First of all, Uber selects its drivers among those who have regularly applied to the company. Secondly, Uber is indispensable for delivering the substantive service offered by its drivers: Without Uber "drivers would not be led to provide transport services and persons who wish to make an urban journey would not use the services provided by those drivers". Finally, Uber exercises a "decisive influence" over the conditions under which that service is provided: It determines at least the maximum fare, it receives that amount from the client before paying part of it to the driver, and it exercises a certain control over the quality of the vehicles, the drivers and their conduct, which can, in some circumstances, result in their exclusion (§ 39). For a first comment, *See, e.g.*, Hacker (2018).

21 A longer explanation for this conclusion can be found in the opinion rendered by Advocate General Szpunar delivered on May 11, 2017, in *Asociación Profesional Elite Taxi v Uber Systems Spain*, § 33–35 ("In the case of composite services, namely services comprising electronic and non-electronic elements, a service may be regarded as entirely transmitted by electronic means, in the

first place, *when the supply which is not made by electronic means is economically independent of the service which is provided by that means* (...) where the provider of the service supplied by electronic means is also the provider of the service not supplied by such means or where he exercises decisive influence over the conditions under which the latter service is provided, so that the two services form an inseparable whole, I think it is necessary to identify the main component of the supply envisaged, that is to say, *the component which gives it meaning in economic terms*"). For the thesis that UberPop just offers an information society service and should not be labeled as transport service, *See, e.g.*, Geradin (2017) ("Uber is not a taxi company. It does not own cars and does not employ drivers. Uber is a software company, which is principally staffed by software engineers").

22 *See* C-104/17, Judgment of the Court (Fifth Chamber) of October 4, 2018, *Komisia za zashtita na potrebitelite v Evelina Kamenova*, ECLI:EU:C:2018:808, par. 38 (Whether a person is acting for 'purposes relating to his trade, business, craft or profession' or in the name or on behalf of a trader, and can be classified as a 'trader', requires a 'case-by-case approach', based on: "whether the sale on the online platform was carried out in an organised manner, whether that sale was intended to generate profit, whether the seller had technical information and expertise relating to the products which she offered for sale which the consumer did not necessarily have, with the result that she was placed in a more advantageous position than the consumer, whether the seller had a legal status which enabled her to engage in commercial activities and to what extent the online sale was connected to the seller's commercial or professional activity, whether the seller was subject to VAT, whether the seller, acting on behalf of a particular trader or on her own behalf or through another person acting in her name and on her behalf, received remuneration or an incentive; whether the seller purchased new or second-hand goods in order to resell them, thus making that a regular, frequent and/or simultaneous activity in comparison with her usual commercial or business activity, whether the goods for sale were all of the same type or of the same value, and, in particular, whether the offer was concentrated on a small number of goods.").

23 Most common requirements are usually regarding professional competence, age, medical fitness, and financial capacity. Cf. Frazzani et al. (2016).

24 No quantitative restrictions exist in Austria, Hungary, Ireland, Lithuania, the Netherlands, Poland, Slovenia, Slovakia and Sweden. Cf. Frazzani et al. (2016).

25 See, e.g., Belgium, Germany, Italy, France, Malta, Poland, Spain and the UK, among others. A single framework is adopted, with some differences, in Luxembourg, Portugal, Slovenia, where the same legislative rules apply to both sectors and, to some extent, also in Ireland and Sweden. Cf. Frazzani et al. (2016).

26 In December 2018, the German Federal Court of Justice (*Bundesgerichtshof*) upheld a lower-court ruling that limousine call service Uber Black, that Uber runs with car rental companies and licensed drivers, could not be resumed because it breaches Germany's 1935 Public Transport Act (*Personenbeförderungsgesetz*) that requires taxis to operate from a concessionary's dispatch office under

local area licenses granted by communal authorities (BGH, December 13, 2018, Docket No. I ZR 3/16, ECLI:DE:BGH:2018:131218UIZR3.16.0, available at https://juris.bundesgerichtshof.de/cgi-bin/rechtsprechung/document.py?Gericht=bgh&Art=en&client=12&pos=0&anz=1&Blank=1.pdf&nr=91770). As in *Uber Spain*, the Court rejected Uber's claim to act only as an intermediary for its drivers and affirmed that Uber breached the obligation that hired cars have to return to a rental firm's main office after carrying out a ride. The German court considered that Uber violates laws reserving taxis the right to wait at the roadside and pick up passengers and thus basically blurs the taxi and rental car services.

27 In February 2015, Estonia amended its *Public Transport Act* ("PTA"). Cf. *Ühistranspordiseadus*, at § 5, available at https://www.riigiteataja.ee/en/compare_original?id=505022016010. In September 2016, Lithuania amended its *Road Transport Code*: Republic of Lithuania, Road Transport Code, Amendments to Articles 7 and 18, September 27, 2016, available at https://www.e-tar.lt/portal/legalAct.html?documentId=32caf3508c8111e6b969d7ae07280e89. Finland had taken a slightly different path by proposing to amend its Act on *Transport Services* (ATS), deregulating the taxi market by abandoning the quota systems for licenses and relaxing conditions to obtain a license, which is the same for any kind of urban transport service (Cf. *Hallituksen esitys liikennekaareksi ja eräiksi siihen liittyviksi laeiksi*, HE 161/2016 vp, available at https://www.eduskunta.fi/FI/vaski/KasittelytiedotValtiopaivaasia/Sivut/HE_161+2016.asp). Portugal had proposed a legislative draft that qualifies intermediation platforms which operate in the field of transport as intermediaries, thus excluding their qualification as service providers. According to the Portuguese proposal, digital intermediaries and drivers using the platforms (so-called TVDE operators) must send a registration form to the *Instituto de Mobilidade e dos Transportes* (IMT) to notify their activity. Similar to the other mentioned cases, drivers are subject to a lighter regime compared to taxis, such as a road training course for drivers and a driver's license for TVDE issued by the IMT (with no quota limitation). Lighter requirements are also requested for vehicles (be less than seven years old; have a maximum of nine seats; be annually subjected to technical inspections; have insurance covering passengers and their losses). Proposta de Lei no. 50/XIII available at: https://www.parlamento.pt/ActividadeParlamentar/Paginas/DetalheIniciativa.aspx?BID=40897.

28 Loi n° 2014–1104 du 1er octobre 2014 relative aux taxis et aux voitures de transport avec chauffeur, JORF No. 0228, October 2, 2014, p. 15,938 (*Loi Thévenoud*). See also Tribunal de commerce de Paris, August 1, 2014, *Association française des Taxis;* Cour d'appel de Paris, November 19, 2015, No. 14/17915; Tribunal de Grande instance de Paris, October 16, 2014; Cour d'appel de Paris, December 7, 2015; Tribunal de commerce de Paris, December 12, 2014; Cour d'appel de Paris, April 5, 2016. Conseil constitutionnel, decision No. 2015–468/469/472, May 22, 2015, Société UBER France SAS et autre; Id., decision No. 2015–484, September 22, 2015, Société UBER France SAS et autre; Id., decision No. 2016–516, January 15, 2016, M. Robert M. et autres

(upholding the ban on UberPop). A New legislation has been adopted in 2016 (*Loi Grandguillaume*, Loi n° 2016–1920 du 29 décembre 2016 relative à la régulation, à la responsabilisation et à la simplification dans le secteur du transport public particulier de personnes, JORF No. 0303, December 30, 2016).

29 Juzgado de lo Mercantil n. 2 de Madrid 22 maggio 2015, https://tinyurl.com/y8qqk56s; Audiencia Provincial de Madrid 23 jan. 2017, https://tinyurl.com/ydccog55.

30 Trib. comm. Bruxelles September 23, 2015, *Radio Taxi Bruxellois v. Uber*, available at https://tinyurl.com/y7dwlfuy.

31 College van Beroep voor het bedrijfsleven 8 dicembre 2014, available at https://tinyurl.com/ycq5zemm.

32 VG Hamburg, August 27, 2014, 5 E 3534/14 and OVG Hamburg, September 24, 2014; VG Berlin, September 26, 2014, VG 11 L 353.14 and OVG Berlin-Brandeburg, April 10, 2015, OVG 1 S 96.14.

33 Tribunale di Milano, May 25, 2015, No. 16612/2015; July 2, 2015, Nos. 35445/2015, and 36491/2015; Tribunale di Torino, sez. I civile, March 24, 2017, No. 1553; Tribunale di Roma, sez. IX civile, April 7, 2017; Id., May 26, 2017, No. 25857.

34 Transport for London, September 22, 2017, https://tinyurl.com/yc6ry6n4 (Uber "is not fit and proper to hold a private hire operator licence"); See also *Aslam v Uber BV*, Employment Tribunal (October 28, 2016), https://tinyurl.com/jyv52p8; Employment Appeal Tribunal (November 10, 2017), available at https://tinyurl.com/y8dxfwgj.

35 When the ECJ rendered its decision, UberPop was operating only in Poland, Czech Republic, Slovakia and Romania.

36 On the law and regulation of sharing mobility, See generally Finck et al. (2020).

37 *See* Opinion of Advocate General Szpunar delivered on May 11, 2017. *Asociación Profesional Elite Taxi v Uber Systems Spain, SL*, § 88.

38 OECD/ITF—International Transport Forum (2016, 7) (arguing that regulators should avoid creating different categories for hire transport providers and indicating that, if differentiations are needed, they should be made explicit, should be substantiated and frequently reviewed).

39 Corte Cost., 26.3.2020, n. 56, https://www.cortecostituzionale.it/actionSchedaPronuncia.do?anno=2020&numero=56.

40 UberBlack provides the service via an app through which the customer request is first delivered to a server run by the digital company that identifies the closest car and contacts the driver while at the same time sending a note to the rental car company. Thus, strictly speaking, the request is not received by the company and then delivered to the driver, as imposed by national rules regulating other categories of urban transport companies other than taxis (rental car companies, private hire vehicles, and so on).

41 *See, e.g.*, AGCM—Autorità garante della Concorrenza e del Mercato (2017), CNMC—Comisión Nacional de los Mercados y la Competencia (2016), ADC—Autoridade da Concorrência (2016), UOKiK—Urzędu Ochrony Konkurencji i

Konsumentów (2016), AZTN—Agencija za Zaštitu Tržišnog Natjecanja (2016) and Komisiya Za Zashtita Na Konkurentsiyata (2015).

42 Such an approach would also entail a mandatory approach for cities of a certain size, according to national standards based on EU guidelines with an Urban Mobility Plans for European cities. Cf. EC—European Commission (2011, para 34); See also Annex I. List of initiatives. 2.3. Integrated urban mobility. 31. Urban Mobility Plans.

43 Cf. Judgment of December 22, 2010, *Yellow Cab Verkehrsbetrieb*, C-338/09, EU:C:2010:814, par. 30 and the case-law cited.

44 Under the subsidiarity principle, the Union must justify the relative efficacy of EU legislation vis-à-vis national or local alternatives. The reasons for concluding that an objective of the Union can be better achieved at Union level shall be substantiated by qualitative and, wherever possible, quantitative indicators. Cf. art. 5, para 3, TUE: "Under the principle of subsidiarity, in areas which do not fall within its exclusive competence, the Union shall act only if and in so far as the objectives of the proposed action cannot be sufficiently achieved by the Member States, either at central level or at regional and local level, but can rather, by reason of the scale or effects of the proposed action, be better achieved at Union level." Art. 5(4) TEU provides that, under the proportionality principle, the content and form of Union action shall not exceed what is necessary to achieve the objectives of the Treaties.

45 Cf. Jean Monnet Project "New Policies and Practices for European Sharing Cities" (EuCity), 586982-EPP-1–2017-1-IT-EPPJMO-PROJECT. The Academic Coordinators of EuCity (Prof. Giorgia Pavani) and Rider (Prof. Guido Smorto) are key staff members of the other Project.

46 As an example, in the US, Uber opposed legal complaints made by disabled users about Uber drivers refusing to put wheelchairs in the car on the grounds that Uber is simply a platform, not a service provider, so that the individual driver is the only responsible for such a prescription. *See* Complaint for Violations of the Americans with Disabilities Act, 42 U.S.C. § 12,101 et seq., the California Unruh Civil Rights Act, Cal. Civ. Code §§ 51 & 52, and the California Disabled Persons Act, Cal. Civ. Code §§ 54–54.3, National Federation of the Blind of California v Uber Technologies, Inc, Case No. 3:14-cv-4086, 52–75 at 14–20 (ND Cal filed September 9, 2014).

47 Directive (EU) 2019/1024 of the European Parliament and of the Council of June 20, 2019, on open data and the reuse of public-sector information, PE/28/2019/REV/1, OJ L 172, poses restrictions to rights on databases but only for public bodies. Yet, access to private-sector data for public authorities is mentioned in EC—European Commission (2017a, b).

48 Further, data sharing and/or pooling may enhance competition, as it may reduce market entry barriers, in particular for small and medium-sized enterprises, minimize the risk of excessive first-mover advantages and increase business opportunities. Cf. EC—European Commission (2018b, 5).

49 On "city experimentation, *See* Lenhardt (2011), Sabel and Simon (2011), Dorf and Sabel (1998) and Lozner (2004).

References

ADC—Autoridade da Concorrência. (2016). *Relatório Preliminar sobre Concorrência e Regulação no Transporte de Passageiros em Veículos Ligeiros*. Available at: https://www.concorrencia.pt/vPT/Noticias_Eventos/ConsultasPublicas/Documents/Relatorio%20Preliminar%20sobre%20Concorrência%20e%20Regulação%20no%20Transporte%20de%20Passageiros%20em%20Ve%C3%ADculos%20Ligeiros.pdf.

AGCM—Autorità Garante della Concorrenza e del Mercato. (2017). *Riforma del settore della mobilità non di linea. Segnalazione 10 marzo 2017*. Available at https://www.agcm.it/dotcmsCustom/getDominoAttach?urlStr=192.168.14.10:8080/C12563290035806C/0/E625CF63D39A5B20C12580E3004C5373/$File/AS1354.pdf.

AZTN—Agencija za Zaštitu Tržišnog Natjecanja. (2016). *Opinion on a municipal decision on the provision of taxi services in Zagreb*. Available at https://www.aztn.hr/en/cca-opinion-on-the-decision-of-the-city-of-zagreb-on-the-provision-of-taxi-services/.

Benkler, Y. (2004). Sharing nicely: On shareable goods and the emergence of sharing as a modality of economic production. *Yale Law Journal, 114*, 273.

Busch, C. (2020). Self-regulation and regulatory intermediation in the platform economy. In M. Cantero Gamito & H. W. Micklitz (Eds.), *The role of the EU in transnational legal ordering: Standards, contracts and codes*. Cheltenham: Edward Elgar.

Caillaud, B., & Jullien, B. (2003). Chicken & Egg: Competition among intermediation service providers. *RAND Journal of Economics, 24*, 309.

CNMC—Comisión Nacional de los Mercados y la Competencia. (2016). *Informe económico sobre las restricciones a la competencia incluidas en el Real Decreto 1057/2015 y en la orden fom/2799/2015 en materia de vehículos de alquiler con conductor*. UM/085/15 y acumulados. Available at https://www.cnmc.es/file/107176/download.

Colangelo, M., & Zeno-Zencovich, V. (2019). *Introduction to European transport law* (3rd edn.) Rome: RomaTre Press.

Davidson, N. M., & Infranca, J. J. (2016). The sharing economy as an urban phenomenon. *Yale Law and Policy Review, 34*, 215.

Dempsey, P. S. (1996). Taxi industry regulation, deregulation & reregulation: The paradox of market failure. *Transportation Law Journal, 24*, 73.

Dillahunt, T. R., & Malone, A. R. (2015). The promise of the sharing economy among disadvantaged communities. In *Proceedings of the 33rd Annual ACM Conference on Human Factors in Computing Systems* (p. 2285). Available at https://dl.acm.org/citation.cfm?id=2702189&dl=ACM&coll=DL&CFID=538559005&CFTOKEN=56128162.

Dorf, M. C., & Sabel, C. F. (1998). A constitution of democratic experimentalism. *Columbia Law Review, 98*, 267.

EC—European Commission. (1985). *White paper. Completing the internal market*. COM (85) 310 final.

EC—European Commission. (2011). *White paper. Roadmap to a single European transport area—Towards a competitive and resource efficient transport system*. COM (2011) 144 final.

EC—European Commission. (2016). *Communication. A European agenda for the collaborative economy*. COM (2016) 356 final.

EC—European Commission. (2017a). *Communication. Building a European data economy*. COM (2017) 9 final.

EC—European Commission. (2017b). *Communication on the mid-term review on the implementation of the digital single market strategy. A connected digital single market for all*. COM (2017) 228 final.

EC—European Commission. (2018a). *Communication. Towards a common European data space*. COM (2018) 232 final.

EC—European Commission. (2018b). *Guidance on sharing private sector data in the European data economy, accompanying the document communication "Towards a common European data space"*. SWD (2018) 125 final.

EC—European Commission. (2020). *Towards a European strategy on business-to-government data sharing for the public interest final report prepared by the high-level expert group on business-to-government data sharing.*
Evans, D. (2003). The antitrust economics of multi-sided platform markets. *Yale Journal on Regulation, 20*, 325.
Evans, D. S., & Schmalensee, R. (2007). The industrial organization of markets with two-sided platforms. *Competition Policy International, 3*, 151.
Finck, M., Lamping, M. Moscon, V., & Richter, H. (2020). *Smart urban mobility. Law, regulation and policy*. Springer.
Fraiberger, S., & Sundararajan, A. (2015). Peer-to-peer rental market in the sharing economy. *University of Chicago Law Review Online, 82*, 116.
Frazzani, S., et al. (2016). *Study on passenger transport by taxi, hire car with driver and ridesharing in the EU. Final report*. Brussels: European Commission.
Geradin, D. (2017). *For a facts-based analysis of Uber's activities in the EU: Addressing some misconceptions*. TILEC discussion paper DP 2017-019. Available at https://papers.ssrn.com/sol3/papers.cfm?abstract_id=2932098.
Hacker, P. (2018). UberPop, UberBlack, and the regulation of digital platforms after the Asociación Profesional Elite Taxi Judgment of the CJEU. Judgment of the Court (Grand Chamber) 20 December 2017, Asociación Profesional Elite Taxi (C-434/15). In *European review of contract law 2018* (p. 80).
Komisiya Za Zashtita Na Konkurentsiyata. (2015). *CPC recommends discontinuing price regulation for taxi services*. Available at https://reg.cpc.bg/Decision.aspx?DecID=300043236.
Lenhardt, R. A. (2011). Localities as equality innovators. *Stanford Journal of Civil Rights & Civil Liberties, 7*, 265.
Lozner, S. L. (2004). Diffusion of local regulatory innovations: The San Francisco CEDAW ordinance and the New York City human rights initiative. *Columbia Law Review, 104*, 768.
McKinsey Global Institute. (2018). *Smart cities: Digital solutions for a more livable future*. Available at https://www.mckinsey.com/industries/capital-projects-and-infrastructure/our-insights/smart-cities-digital-solutions-for-a-more-livable-future.
OECD/ITF—International Transport Forum. (2016). *App-based ride and Taxi services, principles for regulation*. Available at https://www.itf-oecd.org/sites/default/files/docs/app-ride-taxi-regulation.pdf.
Ranchordas, S. (2020). Smart mobility, transport poverty, and the right to inclusive mobility. In M. Finck, M. Lamping, V. Moscon, & H. Richter (Eds.) *Smart urban mobility-law, regulation and policy*. Springer.
Rochet, J. C., & Tirole, J. (2003). Platform competition in two-sided markets. *Journal of European Economic Association, 1*, 990.
Rysman, M. (2009). The economics of two-sided markets. *Journal of Economic Perspectives, 23*, 125
Sabel, C. F, & Simon, W. H. (2011). Minimalism and experimentalism in the administrative state. *Georgetown Law Journal, 100*, 53.
Smorto, G. (2016). The sharing economy as a way to urban communing. *Comparative Law Review*, 1.
Sundararajan, A. (2016). *The sharing economy: The end of employment and the rise of crowd-based capitalism*. Boston: MIT Press.
UOKiK—Urzędu Ochrony Konkurencji i Konsumentów. (2016). *Uber—Statement of UOKiK's position*. Available at https://www.uokik.gov.pl/news.php?news_id=12353.

Shared Mobility in the Process of City-Transport Coevolution: Emerging Geographies and Policy Challenges

Ignazio Vinci

Abstract In the broader context of the relationship between transport and urban development, this chapter discusses the impact that shared mobility services may have on the spatial and functional organisation of cities. In the first section, we review the relationship between transport and urban development in an historical perspective, with a view to the implications that the diverse mobility systems can have on space and the environment. We then examine the cultural and technological drivers for the spreading of shared mobility in contemporary cities, as well as the response these services can provide to different mobility needs in urban areas. In the concluding section, we discuss in what circumstances shared mobility can be part of a policy-making process to promote a balanced urban development, making cities more inclusive and sustainable.

Keywords Shared mobility · Urban development · Space · Sustainability · Planning

1 Introduction

Shared mobility is playing an increasing role in the functioning of contemporary urban areas, especially those of significant demographic size. Its progress is driven by a variety of social, economic and technological factors that we cannot simply reduce to an increased environmental awareness on the part of citizens. For instance, the growth of shared mobility services in recent years would have been impossible without the spread of smartphones connected to the Internet and GPS applications, which enable people and companies to interact easily with each other, taking advantage of unlimited spatial information.

The complexity of these processes in urban areas and the hybrid character of shared mobility systems make it extremely difficult to place these services in the realm of public policy. Since they are often operated by private companies and led

I. Vinci (✉)
Department of Architecture, University of Palermo, Palermo, Italy
e-mail: ignazio.vinci@unipa.it

G. Smorto and I. Vinci (eds.), *The Role of Sharing Mobility in Contemporary Cities*, UNIPA Springer Series, https://doi.org/10.1007/978-3-030-57725-4_3

by the market, the economic viability of shared mobility appears to be as important as its impact in terms of public interest. On the other hand, as they require a certain degree of flexibility to work effectively, their planning and implementation differ significantly from the other planning tools in the hands of local government. In other words, the definition of shared mobility from a public perspective remains rather vague, raising a series of (regulatory) problems for local government as other questions emerging from the overall context of the sharing economy (McLaren and Agyeman 2015; Shareable 2018; Parker et al. 2016; Srnicek 2016).

In this context, this paper explores the different impacts of transport and mobility on the development processes of urban areas, with a view to the approaches and instruments policy-making should consider to increase the role shared mobility can play in making cities more inclusive and sustainable.

After this introduction, the second section analyses the relationship between the transport networks and the physical/functional organisation of cities in a historical perspective. In particular, we describe how urban forms have been shaped by the progress of economic development and, in turn, the ways in which urban morphology can affect the development and organisation of mobility systems. The section ends with a discussion on those contemporary planning paradigms that advocate for a more balanced relationship between transport and urban development, by giving a major role to sustainable mobility in shaping urban form and organisation.

In the third section, shared mobility is examined under the lens of the relationship it creates with cities as an interwoven system of people and places. Going beyond the reductive interpretation of urban space we often find in the transport literature, we explore the territorial dimension of shared mobility, marked by the different interactions between travellers and localities that are established compared to conventional public transport. At the same time, we point out the limits of shared mobility in responding to the needs of a broad range of potential users.

In the final section, we discuss whether (and under which conditions) shared mobility can be employed in policy-making processes to promote sustainable development in cities. In particular, we argue that an effective implementation of shared mobility in urban areas needs policy-makers to consider at least three different planning dimensions: a strategic dimension, an 'urban design' dimension and a management dimension. In the concluding remarks, we highlight the importance of a proper policy design to expand the benefits of shared mobility within contemporary cities, including the empowerment of different local stakeholders and the creation of good governance mechanisms.

2 Transport, Mobility and the Morphologies of Urbanisation

The growth and transformation of urban areas are processes we cannot easily separate from the evolution of their transport networks (Banister 1995). For that reason, this intersection has always attracted huge attention in literature, with contributions ranging from historical perspectives (Hart 2001; Divall and Bond 2003) to the more recent multidisciplinary analyses (Hickman and Banister 2014; Hickman et al. 2015). The relationship between mobility and urban development is extremely relevant to contemporary debate also for its implication on policy-making in modern cities. In fact, since transport is able to affect many aspects of people's everyday life, a mobility policy is increasingly perceived not just as being about ensuring efficient connections between places and inhabitants, but also in terms of the support it can give to cities' socio-economic transition.

Therefore, evolution in the transport sector cannot simply be seen under the lens of technological innovation, but rather as the mirror of deeper cultural shifts, including change in people's lifestyles and the way they interact with/in urban space (Castells 1996; Graham and Marvin 2001; Grieco and Urry 2012; Larsen et al. 2006; Sheller and Urry 2006; Urry 2004).

In contemporary urban areas, it is rather common for inhabitants to live in one neighborhood and to have their job in another, spending free time in a series of other places that have no spatial proximity with home-work locations. What makes these activities accessible in a reasonable length of time is the existence of efficient transport networks, enabling people to move in space with a freedom never known in the past (Bertolini 2012). Behind such increased accessibility to different locations, however, there is a hidden paradox in urban mobility where (especially in the largest cities) people spend more and more time to move than the reason they are travelling for. The essence of this paradox lies in the evolving, often conflicting, relationship economy and society have established with urban space through time history. We can describe this process as a sequence of three main development stages.

The main feature of historical cities, when urban functions were bounded by urban walls, was the prevalence of travel by walking. Despite walking is the least efficient way of moving under a transport rationality, this led to all the economic activities and social interactions being constrained to within a limited spatial range, creating the premises for the main quality we now recognise in Western cities. For instance, this compactness allows the inhabitants of the historic centres of many European cities to satisfy from one to two thirds of their needs by moving on foot or by cycling (Rodrigue 2017).

The balance between socio-economic functions and urban form reached in the pre-modern city was completely subverted by the industrial revolution. During this process, the growing population and increased efficiency of transport brought the first considerable expansion of urban areas, leading to the emergence of a new spatial order within cities. By creating large suburbs outside the limits of historical settlements, urban areas started to assume their current 'polycentric' configuration, characterised by independent urban centres (often shaped on a unique function, i.e. housing) reciprocally connected by extensive transportation systems. In the late stage of this process, when in the second half of the 19th century delocalisation further moved industries away from their original settlements, core urban areas were increasingly transformed into business districts, the accessibility of which became an other powerful driver for the expansion of transport networks (Hansen 1959).

The other relevant phenomenon in the second half of the 19th century is urban sprawl deriving from mass motorisation. Initially, it was determined by the spreading of residential and working activities along the main road corridors from the core to the peripheries of urban areas. Later, when suburbanisation led to saturation of the space between the existing settlements, many of the largest cities started to take on the configuration of urban regions consisting of a multitude of low-density urban centres, partially independent from the core city. Stimulated by other socio-economic processes, such as the desire for a single-family house, urban sprawl had the consequence of quickly reversing the process of functional integration that shaped cities for centuries (Knoacher et al. 2008).

The initial response given by transport culture to these processes was the creation of major highways to connect the suburbs and to enable people to easily reach the city centres. The aim to reduce congestion, however, ended up increasing car-dependency for a large amount of the population, with the rise of journey times and—as argued by Rode et al. (2014)— a shift from a model where accessibility was ensured by 'proximity' to one requiring an increased 'mobility' of individuals in space.

From the 1960s onward, car-dependency rapidly had disrupting effects on urban form, organisation of cities, and the environment. In North American urban areas, it is estimated that the 'spatial imprint' of cars is on average higher than that of house building. In Europe, the surface covered by roads and parking slots ranges between 15 and 20% of total urbanised areas. Considering that cars remain parked for around 98% of their life cycle (Rodrigue 2017), we may conclude that in Western countries driving has turned out to be the less efficient means of transport both from an environmental and economic point of view.

After decades of being associated with crowding and congestion, since the nineties 'urban density' is no longer seen by scholars and policy-makers as a negative attribute for city development. Pioneering regeneration projects in the USA (Calthorpe 1993) showed that reducing the distance between living and working locations, as well as increasing the proximity of places for social interactions, may have a series of positive externalities for urban life, including the benefits deriving from the so-called agglomeration economies (Rode et al. 2014). Many success histories suggest, however, that the density and proximity of functions can have a positive impact on the quality of life only if greater attention is payed to accessibility through sustainable means of transport.

On this basis, in the last thirty years, we have been witnessing the emergence of new planning paradigms seeking to re-conceptualise the density-accessibility nexus in urban areas. The two best known movements in this direction must be referred to the 'Compact City' concept and the 'Transit Oriented Development' approach to city-regional planning.

The Compact City concept first circulated in the USA, where between the eighties and the nineties the *New Urbanism* movement was already playing an active role in fighting the dysfunctions given by the low-density, car-dependent development pattern of North American urban areas (Calthopre 1993). Beyond the different interpretations we can find in literature (OECD 2012), the basic principles of the Compact City concept are: (a) promoting density, proximity, and functional integration as the main qualities in the future development of cities and neighborhoods; (b) planning the concentration of activities in close connection to the public transportation hubs, and (c) creating places characterised by high quality of public space, good accessibility to pedestrians, and great availability of green areas.

Because of their general nature, these principles have been adopted in very different ways in planning practices. In a more normative perspective, the Compact City concept has been understood as a set of standards and techniques for urban designers in order to promote the compatibility between sustainable mobility and the built environment. With reference to other planning scales (i.e. regional dimension), the Compact City concept is often used as the guiding principle for the implementation of long-term urban development strategies, inspired by the reduction of land take, the preservation of rural areas and the concentration of development only in proximity of public transit (de Roo and Miller 2000; Jenks et al. 1996).

These last aims are also central to the planning experiments that can be referred to the *Transit Oriented Development* (TOD) approach (Calthorpe 1993; Cervero 1998; Cervero and Sullivan 2010; Curtis et al. 2009). In Western countries, TOD was first conceived as a method to secure attractivity for new large-scale development projects benefiting from the existence of railway hubs and fast connections to core cities. Later, TOD began to be adopted as a more general approach to combine good accessibility and quality of the environment in a broad range of development projects, even in existing urban areas (Bernick and Cervero 1997; Cervero 1998). Therefore, in a number of urban regeneration projects across the world, the TOD approach focuses not only on increasing connectivity for central places, but also on helping the redevelopment of deprived districts where good accessibility may help socio-economic revitalisation (Curtis et al. 2009).

Both the TOD approach and the Compact City concept have their political roots in the contrast to urban sprawl affecting urban development in Western countries in the second half of the 19th century. Due to rapid suburbanisation processes also in developing countries, however, these principles are becoming the guidelines for local government in a broad range of situations across the world (Bertolini 2012; Pucci and Colleoni 2016; Suzuki et al. 2013). The New Urban Agenda adopted by the United Nations in 2016 identifies 'an appropriate compactness and density in the built environment', as well as 'polycentrism' and 'mixed social and economic uses in built-up areas' among the main planning challenges to prevent urban sprawl, reducing mobility issues and, consequently, to reach the Sustainable Development Goals at a global level (2016).

The growing popularity of these methods in urban planning culture does not mean they can be easily transferred from one local situation to another. In fact, as suggested by Rode et al. (2014), the structure of any urban area is the result of long-term and extremely complex development trajectories, with the result that future development can be affected and in many cases, prevented by a 'path dependency'. In other words, the authors suggest any city is characterised by its own 'urban accessibility pathway', resulting from the way in which the city's organisation and transport networks have co-evolved over time, under the influence of urban form, environmental constraints, and the planning strategies being implemented by local government. For that reason, reshaping the relationship between transport and the built environment may be extremely critical in the short term, requiring enormous investments and implementation periods that are often longer than the time urban functions (especially business activities) require to change their location (Rode et al. 2014).

A number of successful cases across the world, however, demonstrate that the adaptation of mobility systems to urban change (and vice versa) can be more easily addressed by adopting new and proper methodological approaches to local policy. First, as argued by a number of scholars and comparative analyses (Curtis et al. 2009; Suzuki et al. 2013; UN-Habitat 2013), it is important to take an holistic approach both to transport and land-use planning, overcoming the cognitive barriers we often find in local authorities and policy-making. This means, for instance, looking at the mobility problems within urban areas under an integrated perspective that goes beyond the territorial scales and public–private separation (Banister and Marshall 2007; EC 2013; Williams 2016). Secondly, a joint consideration of mobility and urban development can help to maximise the efficiency of the existing transport networks, reducing the need for new infrastructures, especially when technological change (i.e. smart mobility) can effectively address citizens' mobility needs (Flügge 2017; Meyer and Shaheen 2017).

3 Exploring Shared Mobility in a Territorial Perspective

In history, cities are privileged places for sharing a huge amount of goods and services. It is only in the last 20 years, however, that 'formalised' sharing practices started to appear within the mobility sector, becoming a global phenomenon that involves all of the largest cities in Western countries and a growing number of urban areas also in the developing regions (2013). An other relevant process related to the spread of this kind of practice is the diversification of forms and means of transport we can now encompass within the shared mobility concept. In fact, while they were initially limited to the sharing of cars and bikes within limited parts of urban areas, shared solutions are now adopted in various aspects of transportation, including parking (Park-sharing) or freight and logistics (Arcidiacono and Duggan 2019).

As a result, the shared mobility concept now includes a wide range of transport services, targeted to a variety of users and responding to different social demands and business models (Shaheen and Chan 2015). To cite one example, by referring to car sharing, Santos (2018) identifies four different models: (1) peer-to-peer platform, where individuals can rent their cars when not in use; (2) short-term rental of vehicles managed and owned by a provider; (3) companies owning no cars themselves, but signing up ordinary car owners to act as drivers offering a taxi-like service; and (4) on-demand private cars, vans or buses and other vehicles, such as large taxis, shared by passengers going in the same direction. Translating these models into a spatial perspective, according to Cohen and Shaheen (2018), shared mobility services can be distinguished into (a) roundtrip services (motor vehicle, bicycle or other low-speed mode is returned to its origin); (b) one-way station-based services (vehicle, bicycle or low-speed mode is returned to different designated station locations), and (c) one-way free-floating service (motor vehicle, bicycle or low-speed mode can be returned anywhere within a geographic area).

Another interesting definition can be found in Machado et al. (2018), when the authors describe shared mobility as "innovative initiatives based on the 'access to' instead of the 'ownership of', in which individuals share each other's material assets (vehicles, money, etc.), and intangible resources (personal skills, time availability, etc.) in order to provide mobility services to access places" (p. 5). This new relationship established by users among material and immaterial resources allowing transport in urban areas turns them not simply into recipients of a mobility service but into an integral part of a more complex 'mobility system' (Civitas 2016). This relevant transition in the functioning of urban transport is enabled by enormous change in modern society, of which shared mobility is one of the clearest example.

In this respect, Docherty et al. (2018) have argued that the shared mobility services we can find in our cities are basically united by two main features.

- First, to be an expression of that cultural shift, according to which a growing number of individuals is inclined to replace ownership of a vehicle with its temporary use (usership), stimulated by the easy accessibility to services (i.e. booking and payment solutions) and with other advantages offered by public authorities;
- Second, to take advantage of an enormous amount of geo-data and spatial information, partially shared by the same users, able to provide customers a variety of 'context-specific' transport options.

From this perspective, while an explanation for the recent growth of shared mobility lies in a change in social values (i.e. less importance to cars), much more importance has to be given to the disruptive advance in information and communication technology (Rode et al. 2014). Modern shared mobility services are based on the existence of powerful IT platforms, accessible from millions of smartphones connected to the web, that give the system the shape of a virtual network characterised by flexibility, interactivity and unlimited boundaries. By referring to the close relationship established within this network between different mobility operators, geographical data and user interactions, the concept of 'mobility ecosystem' is frequently found in literature (Van Audenhove et al. 2014). In a mobility ecosystem, transport is not meant as a single good/service offered to travellers, but rather as a series of different mobility services, whose integration offers users a wide range of travel options to choose from on a daily basis.

An interesting perspective to understand the impact of technological innovation on transport and, in turn, on the space-mobility relationship is offered by the semantic change underway to the concept of 'accessibility'. Accessibility is defined by Miller (2005) as a multi-faced concept that ultimately centres on an individual's ability to conduct activities within a given environment. The author says that innovation in transport and ICT are drastically changing the relationship among place, space, persons and activities, as these technologies have the power to "shape lives by changing the number and types of activities individuals can experience as well as their distribution in time and space", while on the other hand, they can "shape cities by altering a fundamental reason for urban settlement, namely, accessibility to people activities and opportunities" (Miller 2005, p. 64). As a result, by providing a more efficient combination of demand and supply of transportation, Miller suggests that new technologies are leading to the emergence of a 'people-based' accessibility pattern in addition to a mobility organisation responding to the old 'place-based' paradigm. In other words, while the importance of 'places' such as home and work will not disappear, increased mobility of people in space and time transport should consider an approach that can "accommodate accessibility of people to people as well as people to places" (Miller 2005, p. 73).

A crucial concept to explain such a shift in the approach to transport is the concept of 'Mobility as a Service' (MaaS), firstly developed by Hietanen (2014) after experimental applications in North Europe. A model based on the MaaS notion can be described as a

> door-to-door combination of all transportation modes where a 'mobility aggregator' gathers and sells all services through a single smartphone app, allowing easy fare payment, one-stop billing and the integration of subsidies, if any. Following this logic, MaaS can dissolve the boundaries between different transport modes by providing a customer-centric experience while improving the efficiency of the entire transport system. (Civitas 2016, p. 13)

The emergence of these kinds of mechanisms clearly marks a turning point from an 'infrastructure-based' transport model to a 'user-based' mobility system, a virtual environment where different kind of mobility services are customized to users with flexibility in time and space. This process is extremely relevant to the purpose of this paper, as it is going to completely subvert the relationship between people mobility practices and the functional and material structures of cities. Low and Astle (2009) have pointed out that it is the adaptivity of smart mobility practices that makes modern society less dependent on the settings of old transport systems. In other words, while the dependency on existing physical infrastructures will not disappear in future cities, the emergence of flexible transport instruments such as shared mobility will be able to minimise the impact of their 'fixity' on the citizens' mobility needs.

A crucial role in this process is played—again—by the technology in the possession of travellers, on their being connected to an amount of relevant data to acquire knowledge during their trip. In fact, the availability of geo-data in the hands of moving individuals has drastically changed the relationship between travellers and urban spaces. Traditional places where people used to experience everyday life are flanked by a kind of virtual space, deriving from the dynamic combination of mobility networks, geographical information, interactions with service providers, and other individuals on the move (Castells et al. 2014; Wang et al. 2016).

In this perspective, the way the notion of Socio-Technical System (STS) from Geels (2012) has been adapted to the transport sector by Docherty et al. (2018) is quite interesting. They argue that due to its complexity, the mobility system cannot be explained merely through technological factors. On the contrary, its functioning "comprises technology (e.g. cars and traffic lights), infrastructure (tracks, roads, filling stations and paths), but also knowledge, markets and user practices, cultural and symbolic meaning, policy and institutions, and the industries involved in production and operation" (Docherty et al. 2018, 115). As a result, understanding the transition of the transport sector is not "simply a matter of engineering know how, road design nor policy preference, but also a matter of negotiating social norms, customs and practices" (Docherty et al. 2018, 115).

Of this interaction among social, environmental and technological factors, modern shared mobility appears to be one of the most intriguing (and in some way ambiguous) expression. The added value of these systems, in fact, is creating a bridge between resources of different natures, but not mutually connected. For instance, they take advantage of new technologies (i.e. Internet and smartphones), but could not work without the availability of traditional infrastructures (i.e. roads). From another perspective, most shared mobility systems lie at the intersection of public interest and the market, so that the evaluation of their social impact needs to take account of a huge amount of variables. In other words, shared mobility appears to be the result of a hybridisation of different existing instruments and practices related to mobility, which cannot be investigated solely under the lens of transport culture.

Despite the increasing speculation on the impact of shared mobility on sustainable development, there are still few analyses that take an holistic perspective on these processes. An attempt to describe the potential role of shared mobility in urban areas viewed as complex 'ecosystems' has been recently made by Cohen and Shaheen (2018). In particular, they identify four main domains respect to which shared mobility impact should be evaluated: (1) for its influence on travel behaviours, (2) its impact on the environment, (3) on land use and (4) on the social dimension. Authors also enumerate the policy sectors regarding which such domains should be implemented in urban areas by means of planning instruments. These are:

- Transportation and circulation, since shared mobility can influence travel patterns, such as modal choice, vehicle occupancy and vehicle miles travelled;
- Zoning and growth management, as shared mobility can affect land use–related planning factors, including zoning requirements (i.e. parking minimums), parking demand and the use of public rights-of-way;
- Urban design, given that shared mobility can support sustainability principles by promoting walkability, cycling and public transit use, while reducing the need to own personal vehicles;
- Housing, since shared mobility can support housing strategies by reducing the parking demand and minimum parking requirements of new developments;
- Economic development, as shared mobility can create new opportunities for employment and generate revenue from underused resources;
- Environmental policy, conservation and climate action, given that shared mobility has the potential to reduce negative impacts commonly associated with surface transportation, such as greenhouse gas emissions.

The other side of the coin when approaching shared mobility impacts under such a wide policy perspective is the problem of evaluating its effects on urban development. In fact, the more these domains are interconnected each other, being related to policy affecting both the physical and socio-economic structure of cities, the less easy it is to find evidence to legitimise the role of shared mobility in sustainable development processes. For instance, it is rather unclear how shared mobility can impact on—and, in turn, be influenced by—a series of values of urban areas, such as the quality of the built environment, the higher or lower degree of social cohesion, or the types of economic relations we can find in different neighbourhoods.

The search for an holistic approach to understanding the effects of shared mobility in urban areas, therefore, is more commonly translated into general recommendations or policy guidelines, generally drawn from good practices developed across the world. For instance, it is argued that the major impact from the implementation of shared mobility systems has to be expected in urban areas with a significant amount of population, with a highly differentiated social structure and various functions concentrated in space. The availability of public areas is also mentioned as one of the main drivers for the success of shared mobility implementation, as well as proximity to the public transit hubs, where shared mobility can give solution to the well known first-mile/last-mile (FM/LM) problem for commuters (Civitas 2016).

It is widely agreed, on the contrary, that urban suburbs are the territorial dimension where it is harder to find a balance between the social and economic sustainability of shared mobility services. Analyses on bike sharing (Shaheen et al. 2014 or Stehlin 2019) found that in the marginal districts shared mobility ends up being hindered by the existence of a vicious circle: on the one hand, due to the fewer number of expected users, the location of bike-sharing stations in low-density neighbourhoods turns out not to be effective from an economic point of view; on the other, the scarcity of bikes available makes the service unattractive to other potential users, reducing the returns to a point that even the infrastructure costs of maintenance are generally not covered. In the cases of districts where spatial marginality is combined with social problems, the spread of shared mobility is also prevented by the risks associated to bike theft or the fear that stations could be vandalised (Stehlin 2019). These factors are viewed as serious obstacles also for the spread of the car-sharing market in the suburbs.

This evidence suggests that impacts of shared mobility on urban development processes are not always relevant and they are certainly spatially uneven. This unites shared mobility to other types of (public) policy which require subsidies to work, for instance, the public transport sector. However, if we expect shared mobility to have a more limited impact on local development, it can be an important ingredient of any mobility-led urban strategy. Particularly, it seems to be crucial to increase the sinergy to other mobility systems and with the built-up environment, objectives that can be achieved by giving to planning the multiple dimensions that will be explored in the following section.

4 Why Plan Shared Mobility?

According to the literature (Banister 1995; Divall and Bond 2003; Hansen 1959; Hart 2001; Rodrigue 2017), in the course of mankind's history, we can define the relationship between transport, urban development and city planning as the sequence of the following four main stages.

- In a pre-modern period, until the industrial revolution, the greater part of people's movements took place within the narrow limits of city boundaries, often still defined by their defensive walls (Rodrigue 2017). What we now call 'transport policy' was mainly led by military interests and addressed to ensure the exchange of goods among the main cities and marketplaces. Within urban areas, there was no public transport and therefore no distinction between transport infrastructure and public space. Such a mixture, later seen as a conflict to be removed by the transport culture, resisted in many historical areas of Western (and mostly European) cities, becoming a point of strength in contemporary urban development.
- During the industrial revolution, the concentration of people and factories at the margins of old towns started that process urban scholars later defined a 'fordist' organisation of urban areas (Jessop 1992). As a consequence of urban growth and districts' functional specialisations, the largest urban areas started to assume a polycentric configuration and home-work moves of people to increase both in time and length. Since the beginning of this process, we have witnessed the spread of railroads around and within urban areas, supporting the birth of public transport and later the emergence of transport science as a recognisable body of knowledge to support local government.
- In the second half of the 20th century, large-scale motorisation and the spread of car ownership brought a second disruptive impact to cities' organisation and urban forms (Divall and Bond 2003). The flexibility of private transport and changes in lifestyle (i.e. desire for independent houses) enabled the creation of endless low-density suburbs, often detached from the public transport networks. As a response, the attention of local government was increasingly diverted to major road projects and urban plans influenced by the problem of accessibility to private vehicles, with the consequence of creating a car-dependent urban organisation in most Western cities.
- In the last twenty years, the city-transport relationship can be read as an hybridisation of the mobility systems/practices implemented over the previous two centuries. Despite the fact that urban mobility remains largely dependent on the 'infrastructure capital' inherited from the past, mobility is increasingly affected by new cultural values and societal challenges: a growing sensibility towards the environment (Givoni and Banister 2014; Hickman and Banister 2014), the transition towards a post-industrial organisation of economy and society (Amin 1995; Grieco and Urry 2012), the emergence of new concepts and paradigms to urban mobility and city planning (OECD 2012, 2013). As a result, since the nineties,

local government has turned back to consider the importance of a balanced integration of transport and urban development policy, in the light of new planning methods and innovation in decision-making processes.

To define the role shared mobility can play in contemporary urban policy, we need to consider the legacy of that historical progress, understanding the reasons why transport modes have been replaced by others in response to change in cities' economy and society. In fact, on the one side, shared mobility is a set of practices built on the use of existing—not innovative—transport equipment: material infrastructures like roads or parking areas, or vehicles such as cars or bikes. But on the other, these systems are a genuine example of the complex transition processes urban areas are facing after globalisation, and their diffusion must be read in the wake of the emergence of the so-called platform economies (Parker et al. 2016; Srnicek 2016). Since they are often run by private operators responding to the market, shared mobility services must be viewed as an expression of a range of stakeholders with different rationalities. As a result, they can be placed at the crossroads of the public interest and the market, creating quite a few problems when shared mobility is approached under the lens of public policy. These include questions such as: can shared mobility services be widely distributed in urban areas without providing negative spillovers on the public interest? To what extent can these services be planned and regulated by local government? Is shared mobility able to contribute to urban sustainability beyond transport and mobility goals (i.e. reducing social and geographic marginalities)?

To give an initial response, it is worth returning to reflect on the relationship the various transport systems tend to establish with urban space, which means—in other words—seeking to understand their 'territoriality'. Traditionally, public transport is shaped on the structure of selected infrastructure corridors (i.e. main roads or railways), which make the movement of large amount of urban dwellers faster and cost-efficient. On the contrary, modern shared mobility systems (think for instance to the *free-floating* services) are based on the assumption that it is inconvenient to be bound by the 'fixity' of a given infrastructure. By refusing the constraint of conventional transport networks, shared mobility used to establish a flexible and non-hierarchical relations both with urban space and the other transport systems, creating unexplored challenges to urban planning and city management. These challenges include issues such as regulation, insurance, business models and equity (Civitas 2016). Recognising that the implementation of innovative mobility services usually takes place without any change in the local regulatory framework, many authors have pointed out the risks for the collective interest and claimed greater control from local government. On the one hand, as pointed out by Docherty et al. (2018), one risk is losing control over public space with the consequence of creating conflicts among the different mobility operators and a reduction of citizens' right to mobility. On the other, Machado et al. (2018) have raised a problem of democracy in decision-making, given that access by new shared mobility operators in the local markets often takes place as a result of negotiations, details of which are not made public.

Most of the advantages to plan and regulate shared mobility could arise from a stronger integration both with urban development and the public transport system.

However, in spite of the huge amount of works available on sustainable mobility (i.e. EC 2013, Suzuki et al. 2013, UN-Habitat 2013, Williams 2016 or Bertolini 2017, Givoni and Banister 2014, for a more critical perspective), it is only in recent works such as Civitas (2016) or Cohen and Shaheen (2018) that this integration is treated in an explicit way. In these works, it is argued that shared mobility integration in urban development needs to be promoted by considering three main planning dimensions: a strategic dimension, an urban design dimension and a management dimension.

Under a strategic perspective, it is widely agreed that shared mobility can play a greater role when cities are able to adopt a long-term development perspective, describing how mobility interacts (or should interact) with the functional organisation of different urban areas. In terms of policy-making, it means basically to create a stronger connection among two typical planning functions under the responsibility of municipalities: one is land-use planning, and the other is public transport planning. An attempt to facilitate such cooperation in the European cities can be seen in the 'SUMP approach' developed by the EU, requiring local government to prepare Sustainable Urban Mobility Plans to identify large-scale transport challenges that can be addressed at different scales with the involvement of local stakeholders, including the shared mobility operators (EC 2013).

What we have called 'urban design dimension' refers to the challenge of providing the changes required in the built environment to make shared mobility work best in cities (Cohen and Shaheen 2018). It means that land-use plans and regeneration schemes should include infrastructure of vital importance for the shared mobility systems—i.e. park and ride areas, pick-up stations, bike-lanes or pedestrian areas—without providing conflicts with urban functions or other mobility networks. An additional difficulty to urban design arises when shared mobility has to be placed within districts characterised by density of functions or even by historical values. In that circumstance, a solution suggested in literature is concentrating shared mobility spots within 'public transport hubs' (Civitas 2016), where use of shared means can be stimulated by greater accessibility to other transport systems.

A management approach is particularly required when both the planning and the urban design dimensions do not provide effective solutions to the problem of integrating shared mobility in urban development. For instance, a proper shared mobility management can include a range of measures—including pricing policies, incentives to users or, by contrast, access restrictions to private cars in certain areas—that can play a subsidiary role in stimulating the acceptance of these innovative services (Santos 2018). Other examples include reduced or no fees for shared mobility services to public transport subscribers, as well as discounts to parking costs or free access to restricted zones.

Internationally, there are still more limited policies that seek to include incentives for the shared mobility sector within the implementation procedures of urban development projects. Some US cities, however, are providing reward mechanisms to developers that give space to shared mobility within their construction plans, including the reduction of required parking lots respect to standards. Contracts with the private sector are also crucial when local government is seeking to develop shared mobility in areas with limited market potential. For instance, investments on shared mobility services in marginal neighbourhoods are increasingly required by cities to new operators wishing to enter the more profitable urban areas (Cabanatuan 2014).

The implementation of these policy tools needs to be accompanied by—and often are the expression of—a broader innovation process in local governance. It is agreed in the literature that innovation in urban mobility usually stems from good partnership relations with the relevant stakeholders in the transport sector (2013). This is of critical importance due to the strong asymmetry (in terms of goals, organisation and business expectation) we may find among various mobility operators. On the other side, for the impact change in urban mobility may have on the life of cities, it is essential also to widen the consultation process to local stakeholders outside the small circle of the transport operators. Specifically, decision-making processes should capture the perspectives of those directly involved in the socio-economic transformation of urban areas, including small businesses, housing associations, community leaders and the third sector. Beside that, new mobility schemes would greatly benefit from the implementation of education and communication activities, given that the success of shared mobility is strictly dependent on the ability to change the 'travel behaviours' of potential users.

With regard to the last question, some scholars have pointed out that we still lack widespread knowledge on the (social) mechanisms regulating the shared mobility phenomenon. For instance, Cohen and Shaheen (2018) suggest public policy-makers should require shared mobility operators to make data available on the use of services in urban areas. The availability of these data, it is argued, would be of great importance to achieve two relevant objectives for the public interest: first, by combining data with those available on public transit, local authorities would be in a position to better understand the impact of shared mobility services at different territorial scales; secondly, urban science will be enabled to increase the knowledge on the socio-economic transitions taking place within cities, giving back to policy-makers insight on the mechanisms affecting the mobility-urban development nexus for the near future.

References

Amin, A. (Ed.). (1995). *Post-fordism: A reader*. Oxford: Blackwell.

Arcidiacono, D., & Duggan, M. (2019). *Sharing mobilities: Questioning our right to the city in the collaborative economy*. London, New York: Routledge.

Banister, D. (1995). *Transport and urban development*. London: Spon.

Banister, D., & Marshall, S. (Eds.). (2007). *Land use and transport planning: European perspectives on integrated policies*. London: Elsevier.

Bernick, M., & Cervero, R. (1997). *Transit villages in the 21st century*. New York: McGraw-Hill.

Bertolini, L. (2012). Integrating mobility and urban development agendas: A manifesto. *disP, 188*, 16–26

Bertolini, L. (2017). *Planning the mobile metropolis. Transport for people, places and the planet*. London: Palgrave.

Cabanatuan, M. (2014). Car-sharing firms getting 900 S.F. Street parking spaces. *SFGate*, April 9, 2014. https://www.sfgate.com/bayarea/article/Car-sharing-firms-getting-900-S-F-street-parking-5387271.php.
Calthorpe, P. (1993). *The next American metropolis: Ecology, communities, and the American dream*. New York: Princeton Architectural Press.
Castells, M. (1996). *The rise of the network society: The information age: Economy, society and culture*. Oxford: Blackwell.
Castells, M., Gelernter, D., Vázquez, J., & Morozov, E. (2014). *Change: 19 key essays on how Internet is changing our lives*. Nashville: Turner.
Cervero, R. (1998). *The transit metropolis: A global inquiry*. Washington: Island Press.
Cervero, R., & Sullivan, C. (2010). *Toward green TODs*. Berkeley: University of California.
Civitas. (2016). *Smart choices for cities. Cities towards mobility 2.0: Connect, share and go*! Brussels: Civitas Consortium.
Cohen, A., & Shaheen, S. (2018). *Planning for shared mobility*. Chicago: American Planning Association.
Curtis, C., Renne, J. L., & Bertolini, L. (2009). *Transit oriented development: Making it happen*. Farnham: Ashgate.
de Roo, G., & Miller, D. (Eds.). (2000). *Compact cities and sustainable urban development: A critical assessment of policies and plans from an international perspective*. Aldershot: Ashgate.
Divall, C., & Bond, W. (2003). *Suburbanizing the masses: Public transport and urban development in historical perspective*. Aldershot: Ashgate.
Docherty, I., Marsden, G., & Anable, J. (2018). The Governance of smart mobility. *Transportation Research Part A, 115*, 114–125.
EC—European Commission. (2013). *Developing and implementing a sustainable urban mobility plan. Guidelines*. Bruxelles: Directorate-General for Mobility and Transport.
Flügge, B. (2017). *Smart mobility—connecting everyone: Trends, concepts and best practices*. Springer.
Geels, F. (2012). A socio-technical analysis of low-carbon transitions: Introducing the multi-level perspective into transport studies. *Journal of Transport Geography, 24*, 471–482.
Givoni, M., & Banister, D. (2014). *Moving towards low carbon mobility*. Cheltenham: Elgar.
Graham, S., & Marvin, S. (2001). *Splintering urbanism: Networked infrastructures, technological mobilities and the urban condition*. London, New York: Routledge.
Grieco, M., & Urry, J. (2012). *Mobilities: New perspectives on transport and society*. Farnham: Ashgate.
Hansen, W. G. (1959). How accessibility shapes land use. *Journal of the American Institute of Planners, 35*(2), 73–76.
Hart, T. (2001). Transport and the city. In R. Paddison (Ed.), *Handbook of urban studies* (pp. 102–123). London, New York: Sage.
Hietanen, S. (2014). Mobility as a service—The new transport model? *Eurotransport, 12*(2), 2–4.
Hickman, R., & Banister, D. (2014). *Transport, climate change and the city*. London, New York: Routledge.
Hickman, R., Moshe, G., Bonilla, D., & Banister, D. (Eds.). (2015). *Handbook on transport and development*. Cheltenham: Elgar.
Jenks, M., Burton, E., & Williams, K. (Eds.). (1996). *The compact city: A sustainable urban form?* London: Spon.
Jessop, B. (1992). Fordism and post-fordism: A critical reformulation. In A.J. Scott & M. Storper (Eds), *Pathways to regionalism and industrial development* (pp. 43–65). London: Routledge.
Knoacher, H., Rode, P., Tiwari, G. (2008). How roads kill cities. In R. Burdett & R. Sudjic (Eds.), *The endless city* (pp. 340–347). London: Phaidon.
Larsen, J., Urry, J., & Axhausen, K. (2006). *Mobilities, networks, geographies*. Aldershot: Ashgate.
Low, N., & Astle, R. (2009). Path dependence in urban transport: An institutional analysis of urban passenger transport in Melbourne, Australia (1956–2006). *Transportation Policy, 16*(2), 47–58.

Machado, C., de Salles, N., Berssaneti, F., & Quintanilha, A. (2018). An overview of shared mobility. *Sustainability, 10,* 4342.
Meyer, G., & Shaheen, S. (Eds.). (2017). *Disrupting mobility: Impacts of sharing economy and innovative transportation on cities.* Springer.
Miller, H. (2005). Place-based versus people-based Accessibility. In D. Levinson & K. Krizek (Eds.), *Access to destinations* (pp. 63–89). Bingley: Emerald Group.
McLaren, D., & Agyeman, J. (2015). *Sharing cities: A case for truly smart and sustainable cities.* Boston: MIT Press.
OECD. (2012). *Compact city policies: A comparative assessment.* Paris: Organisation for Economic Cooperation and Development.
Parker, G. G., Van Alstyne, M. W., & Choudary, S. P. (2016). *Platform revolution.* New York, London: Norton.
Pucci, P., & Colleoni, M. (2016). *Understanding mobilities for designing contemporary cities.* Springer.
Rode, P., Floater, G., Thomopoulos, N., Docherty, J., Schwinger, P., Mahendra, A., & Fang, W. (2014). *Accessibility in cities: Transport and urban form.* NCE Cities Paper, 03. London School of Economics and Political Science.
Rodrigue, J. P. (2017). *The geography of transport systems.* London, New York: Routledge.
Santos, G. (2018). *Sustainability and shared mobility models. Sustainability, 10,* 3194.
Shaheen, S., & Chan, N. (2015). *Mobility and the sharing economy impacts synopsis: Shared mobility definitions and impacts.* Berkeley: Transportation Sustainability Research Center.
Shaheen, S., Elliot, A., Martin, W., Chan, N. D., Cohen, A. P., & Pogodzinski, M. (2014). *Public Bikesharing in North America during a period of rapid expansion: Understanding business models, industry trends, and user impacts.* San Jose: Mineta Transportation Institute. Available at https://transweb.sjsu.edu/PDFs/research/1131-public-bikesharing-business-models-trends-impacts.pdf.
Shareable (Ed.). (2018). *Sharing cities: Activating the urban commons.* San Francisco: Tides Center.
Sheller, M., & Urry, J. (2006). The new mobilities paradigm. *Environment and Planning A, 38,* 207–226.
Srnicek, N. (2016). *Platform capitalism.* Cambridge: Polity Press.
Stehlin, J. G. (2019). *Cyclescapes of the unequal city: Bicycle infrastructure and uneven development.* Minneapolis: University of Minnesota.
Suzuki, H., Cervero, R., & Iuchi, K. (2013). *Transforming cities with transit: Transit and land-use integration for sustainable urban development.* Washington: The World Bank.
UN-Habitat. (2013). *Planning and design for sustainable urban mobility: Global report on human settlements 2013.* New York: United Nations.
UN-Habitat. (2016). *New urban agenda.* New York: United Nations.
Urry, J. (2004). *Mobilities.* Cambridge: Polity Press.
Van Audenhove, F. J, Korniichuk, O., Dauby, L., & Pourbaix, J. (2014). *The future of urban mobility 2.0: Imperatives to shape extended mobility ecosystems of tomorrow.* Paris: ADL.
Wang, D., Xiang, Z., & Fesenmeier, D. (2016). Smartphone use in everyday life and travel. *Journal of Travel Research, 55*(1), 52–63.
Williams, K. (2016). *Spatial planning, urban form and sustainable transport.* New York, London: Routledge.

Urban Mobility, Social Inclusion and Participation: A Qualitative Study in Palermo, Italy

Cristiano Inguglia, Martina Di Marco, and Miriam Ricci

Abstract The purpose of this chapter is to discuss the connection between social inclusion and urban mobility, focusing on the role of sharing mobility and to what extent it might be a favourable tool for social inclusion, particularly for disadvantaged groups such as migrants. To our knowledge, whilst the literature has already examined the associations between migrants' social inclusion and mobility, the role of sharing mobility in this process has not yet been widely analysed, especially in the Italian context. Hence, the present chapter addresses this knowledge gap. The rest of the chapter is organised as follows. First, we describe the relationships between mobility and social exclusion, then we consider the case of migrants as a category at risk of social exclusion. We illustrate the connection between sharing mobility and social inclusion using the key findings of a focus group study involving residents and migrants in the city of Palermo. Finally, we discuss the implications for the development of more inclusive sharing mobility services.

Keywords Social inclusion · Sharing mobility · Immigration · Participation · Focus group

1 Mobility and Social Exclusion

Mobility, conceptualised here as physical mobility involving corporeal movement, has an important role in all societies across the world and in different historical times because it enables people to access the necessary resources for surviving and thriving (Stanley and Stanley 2017). In the last few decades, rapid societal transformations have increased the importance of mobility, and the associated transport system enabling it, as a crucial element for accessing services and life opportunities,

C. Inguglia (✉) · M. Di Marco
Department of Psychology, Educational Science and Human Movement, University of Palermo, Palermo, Italy
e-mail: cristiano.inguglia@unipa.it

M. Ricci
Centre for Transport and Society, University of the West of England Bristol, Bristol, UK

G. Smorto and I. Vinci (eds.), *The Role of Sharing Mobility in Contemporary Cities*, UNIPA Springer Series, https://doi.org/10.1007/978-3-030-57725-4_4

making it a key resource for social inclusion (Knowles 2006; Levinson 2010; Lucas 2012; Pereira et al. 2017).

In order to understand the importance of physical mobility for social inclusion, which can be regarded as participation and integration (both actual and perceived) in the life of society as a whole, it is useful to start from the definition of social exclusion. Levitas et al. (2007) have conceptualised social exclusion in a broader way, going beyond the concept of material or economic poverty and referring instead to the lack or denial of goods, services, resources and essential rights that prevent an individual from participation in ordinary activities accessible to the majority of people in the community. Social exclusion has negative effects, both in collective and individual terms. On the one hand, it may damage the sense of social equality and cohesion, and on the other hand, it is negatively associated with the perceived quality of life, and it is also linked to poor psychological and physical health.

Bradshaw et al. (2004) have identified three categories of drivers of social exclusion, which contribute to the intensity of this phenomenon: socio-demographic factors, economics factors and political factors. The first category includes aspects such as ageing, young unemployment and the increase of one-parent families. The second category includes economic factors and trends, such as the decrease in the income of younger and older people, the increase in salary disparity between groups of workers (for example, between women and men), the increase in self-employment as well as precarious, atypical and insecure employment contracts. The last category includes political and policy factors, such as the increase in the gap between highest and lowest salaries, increased costs associated to accessing social and healthcare services and the increase in private property rents (Bradshaw et al. 2004). Other important factors to be considered as potential risks to social inclusion are the personal characteristics of each individual, such as disability, ethnicity, low education levels and citizenship status (Lodovici and Torchio 2015).

Levitas et al. (2007) proposed the operationalization of the construct of social exclusion using a model known as Bristol Social Exclusion Matrix (B-SEM). The model includes all the different aspects that can be both outcomes and risk factors of social exclusion, which are categorised into three key dimensions: resources, participation and quality of life (for a comprehensive description see Levitas et al. 2007).

The link between social exclusion and mobility was explicitly identified and discussed in a landmark policy report by the Social Exclusion Unit (2003), established under the Labour government to better understand the causes and impacts of social exclusion in British society. This report was one of the first extensive evidence reviews to draw attention to the circumstances in which transport, or physical mobility, can act as a barrier to people's access to life opportunities, such as education, employment, health care and social activities. Such circumstances include the lack of personal transport, poor provision of public transport, poor accessibility of transport infrastructure and excessive costs.

A useful concept in this discussion is transport disadvantage (Cass et al. 2005; Currie 2011; Lucas 2012; Ricci 2016; Pucci and Colleoni 2016). This usually concerns situations where the provision of access to and use of the transport system in a broader sense are inadequate or insufficient. A number of factors can contribute to creating transport disadvantage, for example socio-demographic variables such as poverty, disability, ethnicity, gender, age, ill health, characteristics of the transport system itself (such as cost and the quality and level of service), factors related to geopolitical conditions (such as population density) and social obligations.

Lucas (2012) has warned against considering transport disadvantage and mobility-related social exclusion as synonymous. In fact, individuals can be socially included despite an ineffective transport system, or, conversely, they can effectively move and access transport despite living in situations of social exclusion. The author proposes a complex theoretical framework to describe the phenomenon of transport-related social exclusion. In her perspective, social disadvantage, which is determined by a set of factors (such as unemployment, low income and poor housing conditions), interacts with transport disadvantage, for example the lack of personal transport or expensive public transport fares. The result of this interaction may lead to the inaccessibility of key services and life chances, such as social interactions, education opportunities, health care, decent employment, social capital, decision making and so on. This inaccessibility produces, in turn, social exclusion, which can further exacerbate the very factors that determine social disadvantage in a vicious circle. Moreover, the overall process by which transport-related social exclusion is produced and reinforced is also influenced by the action of other factors, such as social and economic norms and trends as well as government policies (Lucas 2012).

More recently, Schwanen et al. (2015) have criticised the tendency in much of the extant academic and policy literature to conceptualise social exclusion as a binary notion which operates through dualism (i.e. between the excluded and the included) and homogenisation (e.g. by overlooking any differences in gradations of exclusion/inclusion). Therefore, they propose to consider social exclusion as multi-dimensional, dynamic, multi-scalar and cumulative process in its effects on people's lives, which can be referred to both groups and single individuals. In this perspective, they describe social exclusion as the "lower levels in the evolving hierarchies of access to, participation in and autonomy with respect to" (p. 125) the different domains that make up the life of a society, such as economic aspects (such as employment and financial resources), political aspects (such as participation in political decisions and the governance system), social aspects (community activities and interpersonal relations), cultural aspects (such as artistic activities and digital media services) and health aspects (both physical and mental).

2 Categories at Risk of Social Exclusion: The Case of Migrants

The extant literature on this topic points out that some categories of people are at higher risk of social exclusion than others, for example older people, young people, people with disabilities, low-income people, women and migrants (Currie and Delbosc 2011; Stanley and Stanley 2017).

A study of social exclusion at European level (Lodovici and Torchio 2015) identified frequent risk factors of social exclusion, such as low-income, disadvantaged work conditions, low level of education, residing in suburban or deprived areas and being an immigrant. According to the study, having a migrant background increases the risk level of marginalization because migrants are more likely to be discriminated against and, as a result, tend to live in disadvantaged areas and to have less access to educational, social and health services, as well as to adequate employment.

This result is confirmed by Price and Chacko (2012) who explored the life conditions of migrants in different countries across the world. They highlight several problems migrants face when they live in foreign countries. Unemployment, unsafe work conditions, poverty, the lack of residence permit, limited access to educational and health services are factors that taken together may negatively affect migrants' active participation in social, economic and politic life, hindering a successful inclusion process (Berry and Sam 2013). This risk is increased by further constraints to accessing transport (both public and private) because of language issues (e.g. difficulties in reading and communicating), difficulties in wayfinding, and the lack of economic resources necessary to acquire a driving license, to buy a private car or pay for public transport fares.

According to Berry (1997, 2005) and Berry et al. (2002), migrants' social inclusion is strongly affected by the process known as psychological acculturation, that is the set of cultural and behavioural changes resulting from prolonged contact between people from different backgrounds. Four outcomes of the acculturation process have been identified: integration, separation, assimilation and marginality (for a comprehensive description see Berry 2005). Here, we focus in particular on the concept of integration, which reflects migrants' desire to maintain their own culture whilst, at the same time, adopting the cultural norms of the dominant or host culture. Integration is frequently associated with better outcomes in terms of adaptation into the host society and better social inclusion (Berry 2017; Berry and Wilcox 2018; Inguglia and Musso 2015; Inguglia et al. 2017).

Therefore, enabling migrants to move around can help them access important goods and services offered by the host country and increase their opportunities for participation and inclusion within their new life context. For example, migrants who have the effective opportunity to access existing mobility services can benefit from a variety of services related to formal and informal education, health, employment and social activities.

However, migrants can and do experience a number of barriers in the host country, which affect how much mobility they can enjoy and, as a result, what services and life opportunities they can access, with negative impacts on their overall inclusion and well-being (Mattioli 2017; Ricci 2017; Pucci and Colleoni 2016; Maddrell et al. 2016). Examples of such barriers include low incomes and material deprivation, inability to speak the language of the host country, lack of knowledge and awareness of how society is organised including rights, entitlements and obligations, lack of awareness of what services are provided and how to access them and more insidious social evils such as racism and discrimination.

Welsch et al. (2018) examined the travel behaviour of migrant people in several countries and compared it to the mobility behaviours of the resident population. They found that migrant people tend to use public transport more than the resident population, particularly in the Netherlands and Austria compared to other countries, and are less likely to own and use bicycles and private motorised vehicles (particularly women). The reliance of migrants on public transport, therefore, can pose significant challenges to their successful inclusion in situations where public transport provision is inadequate. Furthermore, a growing body of evidence indicates that travel behaviour is strongly influenced by socio-demographic characteristics such as income (with low-incomes associated with less mobility, both in terms of trips undertaken and distance travelled), family structure (with larger families experiencing more difficulties with being mobile and accessing services) and education (higher levels are associated with more mobility).

Because migrants are more at risk of poverty and marginalisation, the European Union (EU) promotes, through policies, strategies and research programmes, the creation and strengthening of the opportunities and resources necessary for the full participation of migrants into the economic, social and cultural life of their host countries, to ensure they enjoy an appropriate standard of living and overall well-being in line with that of the resident population. To fulfil this ambition, the EU has developed specific social policies and programmes benefitting the most vulnerable, for example by supporting members states to make public transport systems more efficient, affordable and accessible for all. Support to public rather than private means of transport can also be considered part of a broader strategy to shift travel behaviours to more sustainable forms of transport, especially in the light of global emergencies such as climate change and air pollution.

In this context, it is helpful to explore the potential contribution of a particular type of mobility (Sharing Mobility) to increasing accessibility and social inclusion (Clark and Curl 2016).This will be the focus of the following sections.

3 Sharing Mobility and Social Inclusion

Sharing mobility (SM) can be considered part of a larger phenomenon, the so-called sharing economy, which involves sharing and accessing rather than owning assets of different types. This process of sharing is usually sanctioned by a market transaction. SM involves in particular the sharing of transport assets in space and time by several users, who can access the shared means of transport (e.g. bicycles, vehicles, etc.) alone or with people known to them, or share the ride in the same vehicle with strangers, depending on the specific SM service under consideration (Parkhurst and Seedhouse 2019). Examples of SM include large bike sharing schemes increasingly available in cities around the globe (like Ofo or Mobike), car sharing or car clubs where pools of vehicles can be accessed by paying members and used within a certain specified geographical area (like car2go or Enjoy), and ride-sharing services such as BlaBlaCar. SM services can be delivered by a combination of public bodies, private companies as well as private users (operating as peer-to-peer) (Giacon 2018).

Sharing mobility is underpinned by the massive use of technologies, through digital platforms that control both supply and demand, offering advantages in terms of costs, efficiency and safety. The platform protects and guarantees the security of exchanges among users and controls each process, sanctioning any misconducts (Smorto 2018). The diffusion of digital platforms, easily accessible on the move via smartphone applications, have led to more effective SM systems that are used by a growing customer base.

Another feature of SM is the potential for environmental sustainability because sharing transport assets, such as vehicle fleets that are generally more efficient and cleaner than privately owned cars, can contribute to reduce pollutant gas emissions (Midgely 2009). In addition, if SM services were part of a strategy to significantly reduce motorised traffic in cities, the benefit associated with the increased quality of the urban environment would positively affect people's physical and psychosocial well-being (Hiscock et al. 2014). An increase of wellbeing, in turn, improves people's quality of life, which is related to the standard of comfort experienced by people as a result of improved environmental conditions and positive personal features (Pacione 2003). Finally, sharing systems can be extremely flexible and fit for people's needs. For instance, differently from fixed-route conventional public transport, they allow people to book a car, bike or scooter for customised routes at any time of the day.

According to the Italian Observatory of Sharing Mobility (Osservatorio Nazionale sulla Sharing Mobility 2018), there are some key differences between SM and traditional on-demand services. These include the possibility to establish relations between users regardless of physical or time barriers, the interactive nature of the underlying technology, which allows users to modify aspects of the service in real time according to their own needs, and the collaboration among users not only for commercial purposes.

Some of the most important positive characteristics of SM are linked to the concept of sharing, for example sharing the ride gives people the opportunity to meet others and create new relationships (Currie and Stanley 2008). This applies to SM services such as BlaBlaCar which involve a small group of often like-minded people sharing a vehicle.

Arcidiacono and Pais (2017) analysed the relational and social effects on users of a BlaBlaCar service through individual interviews. Participants in the study expressed satisfaction with their sharing mobility experiences as well as with the people met during these experiences, by using positive adjectives (such as pleasant, social, open and kind) to describe other users. Half of respondents reported having further contacts with their travel mates as well as organising other journeys with them. Additionally, almost 30% of participants declared that they established friendships with their travel mates, whilst 80% reported feeling a common sense of belonging to the new community of BlaBlaCar users.

In the light of evidence from this and other similar research studies (Andreotti et al. 2018; Parigi and State 2014; Schor et al. 2016), SM may have an inclusive potential and it may contribute to improving the quality of life of disadvantaged categories of people, given that they often do not own or have access to a private vehicle. On the one hand, SM tailored to the specific needs of disadvantaged groups may allow people on low incomes to save money and, on the other hand, the community aspects of SM services, such as exchanging ideas and feedback with others, may promote a sense of being socially included. If specific SM services were designed for migrant people, these could facilitate the acculturation process towards integrative outcomes. However, it is essential to make two considerations. The first is that SM services need to be designed for and tailored to the sensibilities and needs of disadvantaged groups to be able to be effective for their social inclusion (see Ricci 2015 for further discussion on this point). The second is that, for SM services to be able to play a significant contribution towards the successful integration of migrants and to benefit other less advantaged sections of the population, they need to be part of a suite of interventions across various policy domains (e.g. education, employment, social care, etc.), whose collective common goal is the social inclusion of more marginalised social groups, or groups that are more at risk of social exclusion and isolation.

4 The Qualitative Study

This section presents the findings of a qualitative study carried out by a research team in the Department of Psychology, Educational Science and Human Movement, University of Palermo (Italy), within the project "Regulating and Deregulating Sharing Mobility in Europe" (RIDER), funded by the Jean Monet programme. The project, running from September 2018 to August 2020, aims at providing recommendations to local policy makers, municipalities and transport authorities for the development of new and improved policies, regulations and business models for sharing mobility, taking into account its impacts on urban spaces, social inclusion, and sustainability.[1]

The main objective of the qualitative study was to discover and analyse the connections between mobility and social inclusion among migrants and Italian nationals living in Palermo, exploring the potential role that sharing mobility services may offer in this context. A further objective was to provide an opportunity for public engagement on this topic, by actively encouraging research participants to offer their own ideas, reflections and proposals in relation to how SM services could be used to improve the quality of life of socially disadvantaged people.

Palermo, the regional capital of Sicily, is one of the biggest cities in Southern Italy. In n 2019, the core metropolitan area of the city has a population of around 663.400.[2] According to the Italian National Institute of Statistic, in 2017, Palermo was one of the Italian cities with the highest deprivation rates (the poverty rate for families is 7.3%).[3] The number of legal immigrants who are permanent residents in Palermo is about 30,000 in 2019. With regard to the public transport system, Palermo has a metro railway service that has just one line. Moreover, it has a public bus system which covers a net area of 340 km with about 90 different routes (the average time people wait at a stop or station for public transit is 23 min[4]). Finally, it has a public tram system completed in 2015 with 4 lines. According to Italian Automobile Club (ACI), in 2017, car ownership level in Palermo was in line with the Italian average (about 59%) but higher than the European average (49.8%) (Bertuccio and Piras 2018). This figure becomes higher if motorcycles and scooters are also included. Use of public transport and bicycles is very low compared to other Italian cities. According to the Euromobility report (Bertuccio and Piras 2018), it is difficult to retrieve data about the use of local sharing mobility services such as Amigo (car sharing) and BiciPa (bike sharing). The key challenges of the mobility system in Palermo are: traffic congestion, low frequency of public transport serving the outskirts, waiting times for public transport, negative public attitudes towards the use of sustainable forms of mobility, the inadequacy of cycle lanes and poor driving behaviour posing significant safety risks to other road users, especially cyclists and pedestrians.

4.1 Methodology

4.1.1 Participants

Thirty-four people ($M = 20$, $F = 14$) living in Palermo (Italy), aged from 17 to 40 years, took part in the research. Among these, 18 had foreign origins and 16 had Italian citizenship. People with foreign origin came from several African countries (Morocco, Senegal, Mali, Gambia), European countries (Spain, French, Romania) and one from the USA. They had been living in Palermo for different periods of time, ranging from a few months to a few years. Many of them lived in the city centre (the old district), a few lived in less central neighbourhoods, and a minority lived in small satellite towns outside the metropolitan area. All participants had a good competence in the use of the Italian language.

4.1.2 Data Collection/Generation Strategy

Participants were recruited with the support of several Non-Governmental Organisations operating in the field of promoting social inclusion. Three focus groups were carried out from February to April 2019 each involving from 10 to 12 participants. Each focus group lasted for 2 h. A facilitator from the University of Palermo conducted each focus group with an independent observer. A focus group protocol, including the list of questions to ask, was developed in order to explore the themes of interest. According to the protocol, the first part of the focus group discussion explored participants' perceptions of mobility in the locality where they lived, looking in particular at the connection between mobility and social inclusion, as well as participants' experiences with and opinions of the urban transport system. Then, the discussion focused on participants' understanding of the concept and applications of SM, to collect information on the real experiences of participants with this type of alternative mobility. At the end of the focus group meeting, participants were asked to provide ideas and suggestions on possible ways to deploy SM services to improve social inclusion in Palermo. Each focus group was digitally audio-recorded and later transcribed in full for analysis (Krueger 2006).

4.1.3 Data Analysis

The qualitative data generated in this study (i.e. the focus group transcripts) was analysed using the constant comparative analysis approach (2001). Each transcript was analysed independently by identifying the main themes, that were labelled with a key word or code, as Jasper (1994) suggested. Subsequently, each transcript was compared with the other ones to identify common themes. The coding strategy and process had been agreed by the researchers before data analysis could commence.

4.2 Results

From the data analysis of the focus group transcripts, six key themes concerning both mobility and sharing mobility have been identified. These are: mobility and well-being, inefficient public transport provision, safety, costs, strengths and weaknesses of sharing mobility. These themes are presented and discussed in depth in the following sections.

4.2.1 Mobility and Well-Being

In relation to the first theme, the possibility to move around without obstacles, safely and via an effective transport system are associated, in people's views, with a perception of well-being. On the contrary, obstacles to people's mobility, such as the lack of the means of transport or of the resources which do not allow people to move freely, bring them to feelings of inadequacy, dissatisfaction and helplessness that are negatively associated with general well-being. For instance, a participant (Male, 35, Moroccan) stated: "If I think I cannot move around, I feel bad… Not to be able to reach every place make me feel in a sort of open-air prison". Another one (Female, 25, Italian) reported that: "If I think I cannot freely reach different parts of my city and I cannot access opportunities, I feel as I cannot live! Life becomes stale, I get into a bad mood and I lose the will to do things".

In this perspective, the focus group interviews confirmed that mobility is represented as a key aspect of social life. It is considered essential for experiencing high levels of life satisfaction: "My life has qualitatively changed since I have my scooter, that allows me to do everything I want" (Female, 20, Italian).

Moreover, in participants' narratives, mobility is connected to the possibility to access social opportunities (for instance, during leisure time) or to attend job-related activities: “I can do my work shifts and then go out for a party in the same day thanks to my car” (Male, 30, Italian) and “If you do not have private means of transport, you will likely have no friends” (Male, 36, Italian).

4.2.2 Inefficient Public Transport Provision

The second theme raised by participants concerns the poor quality of the urban public transport system, which people experience as a real barrier to their mobility. Participants discussed the inefficiency of urban public transport in terms of the following three key issues, or sub-themes: time, geographical availability and Infrastructure.

First, all the participants expressed criticism of the public transport system due to inefficiencies related to time schedules: “Sometimes you have to take public transport to reach certain destinations and that can waste a lot of your time!” (Male, 17, Gambia). The daily routines of participants are negatively affected by problems with punctuality ad reliability, for example when there are delays in the bus schedules and passengers are not kept informed about the situation: “It is very frustrating to wait for a bus more than one hour without any news” (Female, 25, Spanish). These inefficiencies lead participants from different countries to find alternative solutions, avoiding the use of public transport: “We prefer walking rather than waiting hours for a bus. We start walking from a bus stop to the next one and finally we arrive to our destination before the bus has come” (Male, 17, Senegal).

The second subtheme is about inefficiencies in the provision of public transport across the geographical area under consideration. What emerged from the focus groups was the stark difference between the level of service in the more central areas of the city and that in the outskirts. Fewer and less frequent bus routes serving the suburbs lead residents in these areas to feel isolated and disconnected from the city: “When people living in the outskirts go to the city centre, they often say ‘I go to Palermo’, despite the fact that they live in the same town” (Female, 34, Italian) or “I live in outskirt and it is impossible for me to reach the city centre by public transport, because the metro station is very far and the service is infrequent” (Female, 30, Italian). This inefficiency undermines the capability of people living in the suburbs to take part in social activities organised in the city centre as well as to go to work.

The third subtheme is related to inefficiencies in the resources and infrastructures supporting the public transport system: “A few months ago, the bus service has been suppressed, it doesn’t exist anymore. Now I don’t know how I’m going to be able to reach my usual destinations” (Male, 28, Italian). Similar difficulties were also reported with regard to the use of bicycles because of poor provision of cycle lanes and other cycling resources and infrastructure: “If I want to cycle, there are no cycle lanes and riding in the middle of the traffic is very dangerous” (Female, 33, Polish).

4.2.3 Safety

The third theme emerged from the focus groups concerns a more individual and subjective dimension than the previous ones: perceived urban safety, which can be a significant obstacle to achieving quality of life in the community. This theme is divided into two sub-themes: road safety and personal safety, including gender-related issues.

With regard to road safety, participants reported a lot of near-miss experiences in which they were at risk to be run over by buses or cars, whilst they were riding their bikes: "I risked my life three times this week. A bus brushed against me whilst I was cycling. Scooters have got no respect for cyclists. Cars do not even stop at pedestrian crossings! I actually have to raise my arm in order to get them to slow down" (Female, 34, Italian). Participants reported similar negative perceptions of road safety concerning walking: "To reach the tram stop I have to walk along a dark road and I do not feel safe because cars travel very fast" (Female, 38, Italian).

The perceived lack of safety, moreover, is also related to gender issues that cause differences in the ability to use public transport system between males and females. For instance, these differences are related to the use of buses or other transport means in the evening and after dark, when female participants declare they do not feel safe on buses: "I am scared to use public transport in the evening because I am a woman, so I do not use public transport after a certain time" (Female, 30, Italian).

Generally, female participants tend to have a more negative attitude towards using public transport after having negative experiences: "Once I was verbally harassed on a bus so I don't feel comfortable on public transport and avoid taking the bus" (Female, 25, Spanish).

4.2.4 Costs

The fourth theme is related to the costs associated with acquiring and maintaining a private vehicle or using public transport: "The main problem (about having a car) is money. How do I buy petrol? How do I maintain my car? I remember 10 Euros worth of petrol per day, parking charges, tickets, car tax, servicing and all the things that weigh on my parents and me" (Male, 35, Moroccan). Many immigrant participants complained about the costs associated with acquiring a driving licence: "Many of us do not have a driving license because we must take driving lessons and it is too much expensive for us" (Male, 20, Gambia). These financial issues are also raised in relation to public transport and taxi services: "Paying the same ticket valid for 90 min just for a 2 min bus ride is unfair" (Female, 20, Italian) or "Taxis are too expensive and sometimes, if you are not from Palermo, taxi drivers can overcharge you!" (Female, 35, Italian).

4.2.5 Strengths of Sharing Mobility

The fifth theme emerging from data analysis comprises all the comments made by participants on the strengths and the potential contribution of sharing mobility. With regard to this topic, first the participants were asked to produce a definition of SM. Then, the facilitator explained that SM is a transportation strategy based on the shared use of vehicles or other means of transport, that is flexible and customizable, and often use digital platforms. This definition was in line with the descriptions of many participants, although the migrant minors ($N = 5$) who participated to the focus groups showed themselves very surprised by this concept, laughing and asking for further clarification. After a brief explanation, they showed to understand the meaning of the concept even though they never used these services. Among the participants, 10 have already used SM services (mainly bike sharing but also car sharing), whereas 24 never used them (all the 18 persons of foreign origins and 6 Italians). Most participants expressed favourable views about sharing mobility services, especially for its potential benefits towards social inclusion: "The sharing of transport assets is a beautiful idea, it gives you autonomy and the opportunity to save money by sharing the costs among users" (Male, 27, Italian). It is seen as "a type of mobility that creates opportunities to meet other people" (Female, 28, Italian) especially when is based on pooling of means of transport: "Car pooling is a good idea! We can save money and travel together at the same time" (Male, 20, Senegal). In this sense, the concept of sharing mobility, with its potential advantages in terms of saving money and improving social inclusion, is considered a possible solution, which could overcome the weaknesses of the traditional mobility system, which are presented in the previous section.

4.2.6 Weaknesses of Sharing Mobility

Despite all these strengths and potential advantages, sharing mobility is also represented, in the perceptions and experiences of participants, in terms of its disadvantages and weaknesses. These can be articulated into the following four sub-themes: costs, image, digital literacy, geographical availability.

Most of our participants complained that accessing sharing mobility services is prohibitively expensive, due to high fees and restrictive conditions, such as the requirement to have a credit card, which is a barrier for many people: "I would like to use it (the car sharing service), but it is necessary to have a credit card and I do not have one" (Male, 35, Moroccan) or "I would have liked to use the bike sharing service but when I learned about its costs, I decided not to" (Male, 17, Mali). The problems related to the costs of sharing mobility services preclude its use to people at risk of social exclusion. In particular, for the Amigo car sharing service, an annual subscription fee of 25.00 Euros is requested, and then users must pay from 2.00 to 3.00 Euros per hour, whereas BiciPa, the bike sharing service of the municipality, requires an annual subscription fee of 25.00 Euros and a rate from 1.00 to 2.00 Euros per hour. Moreover, the bus ticket for 90 min costs 1.40 Euros, even though there is a high rate of evasion and a high percentage of people (from 20 to 30%) travel without paying bus fares.

When sharing mobility systems are not designed and operated with social inclusion in mind, their potential benefits for socially disadvantaged people, such as migrants, will not be realised in practice: "Is it necessary to have a credit card? It is not a democratic and inclusive service!" (Male, 20, Gambia) or "Although I do understand why sharing mobility services require the use of a credit card, this does not lead to social inclusion. I feel excluded" (Male, 30, Italian).

The second sub-theme is about the Image associated with the users of certain sharing mobility services. Some participants reported having received some criticism from friends and other people because they have chosen to replace their private vehicles with sharing mobility services: "When I told people that I have started to use the bike sharing service instead of my car, they labelled me as a loser and a beggar" (Female, 33, Italian). Most people in Palermo have little awareness and knowledge of sharing mobility services, and this may lead to holding negative preconceptions about sharing mobility and its users: "I have chosen to sell my car and travel using the car sharing service. So my friends have asked me if I have financial difficulties and I need help because of my choice" (Male, 40, Italian).

The third sub-theme is digital literacy. As we have discussed in the previous section, one of most important characteristic of sharing mobility is related to the digital dimension of these services, for example the use of digital platforms to access and manage such services. This aspect could be considered as a strength (because of its convenience and efficiency) but also a barrier for those people who do not have adequate digital skills (for instance older people and particular groups within immigrant communities). Our participants reported a few problems related to the difficulties of accessing the digital platform: "Sharing mobility services need to be accessed through digital platforms but when a user does not have enough digital skills, he or she is cut out!" (Male, 32, Italian). Particular groups in society, such as people who do not speak the language used on these platforms or have difficulties related to age or level of education, are more likely to lack the necessary resources and digital literacy levels to use such services: "In disadvantaged areas web connectivity can be very limited and some people do not have the basic digital skills to access sharing mobility platforms" (Male, 20, Italian). Digital connectivity and literacy are only part of the problem, with other aspects of social, cultural and economic disadvantage combining together to create barriers to social integration and inclusion:" When I arrived in Italy, I had trouble finding my way around because I did not know the Italian language, the city and its streets, and also because I was not able to use the digital application for mobility" (Male, 20, Ghana).

Finally, with regard to the sub-theme geographical availability, participants indicated that the infrastructure supporting sharing mobility services (such as parking bays, shared bike racks) are only provided in certain parts of the city and do not reach several districts in the city outskirts, similarly to what happens for public transport: "The bike racks are only provided within a restricted area of the city" (Male, 40, Italian). Participants who live in the central Old Town and use sharing mobility services consider themselves "special or favoured" compared to those who live in the outskirts, because of the lack of SM and other important transport infrastructure: "I can use Bike Sharing because I have the blessing of living in a central area" (Female, 35, Italian) or "You can access certain services only because you live in privileged areas" (Female, 20, Italian).

5 Conclusions

Our study has confirmed that mobility is a fundamental enabler of personal well-being as well as participation in socio-economic and cultural life (Jain and Guiver 2001; Lucas 2012; Ricci et al. 2016). The findings from our research show how significant this is for people, such as migrants, who are particularly at risk of social exclusion.

Our participants perceived the possibility to safely and effectively move around the city as an essential dimension of their quality of life, subjective well-being and social inclusion. When discussing the role of mobility in their daily lives, our participants identified several aspects of the urban transport system which they perceived as obstacles to accessing life opportunities. These include financial considerations, such as the cost associated with maintaining a private vehicle and acquiring a driving license in a car-dominated society where access to amenities and services is made more convenient to those who drive. Other important considerations concern the inadequacy of the public transport system, which was perceived to be unreliable, unsafe (especially for women) and unable to effectively connect different parts of the city, thus providing poor value for money. This was particularly problematic for migrants who are more likely to have low incomes, live in the outskirts of the city (often in social housing and shelters) and lack access to social, cultural and economic capital. Infrastructure for active mobility, such as walking and cycling, and the overall streetscape was also perceived to be inadequate and unsafe.

Participants' representations of sharing mobility (SM) and its inclusive potential, both in terms of access and connecting to other users, were very positive, even though many of them had never used SM services. However, most participants, especially migrants, were not aware of the SM services operating in the city of Palermo, whilst those who knew about them felt they could not use them because of inaccessible procedures (because of language barriers and lack of digital skills), eligibility requirements and price structure. The existing evidence on SM mobility services, such as car clubs and bike sharing, suggests that these are "niche services", targeted at and accessible predominantly to a small section of the population who is already financially, culturally and socially privileged—typically young male professionals living or working in central urban areas (Clark and Curl 2016; Ricci 2015). A particularly significant obstacle to the inclusive nature of SM services concerns its reliance on the use of "smart" digital technology. Whilst in theory this should enhance the user experience, making travelling (including planning and paying for it) easier and more convenient, in practice it can create barriers to those more at risk of social exclusion, precisely because the services are not designed with their needs in mind.

Furthermore, even when the system of urban mobility allows people to access life opportunities and thus contributes to their social inclusion, this may still be problematic in terms of impact on public health, through air pollution and sedentary lifestyles, and the environment, through CO_2 emissions, traffic congestion and car-dominated urban spaces (Pucher and Buehler 2010). For example, in the case of SM services, if trips on shared cars replace those on more sustainable transport modes, or are generated from latent demand, this can add to congestion, pollution and emissions.

In summary, SM might be a tool for fostering social inclusion and integration of those people who experience transport disadvantage if the services provided are developed for this objective and, at the same time, taking into account the need to promote sustainable lifestyles.

A final consideration concerns proposals to make future SM services more inclusive (Kodransky and Lewenstein 2014). Our participants made the following suggestions. Firstly, it would be necessary to offer a range of SM services with varying prices according to users' incomes, with a system of benefits for low-income people and socially- disadvantaged categories such as migrants. Secondly, the provision of public and private SM services should be enhanced in the outskirts of city, where public transport services are insufficient. Thirdly, it would be useful to introduce integrated subscriptions to incentivize SM service users to utilise also public transport to undertake part of their journeys or other trips, according to their needs. Other suggestions from our participants concern the need to find alternative and more inclusive tools than credit cards to access SM services; and to make SM platforms more accessible to people who do not speak the language of the host country and may lack the digital skills to use them; and to raise awareness of these more socially inclusive services by connecting and communicating with the communities of potential users. Participants suggested that community transport might also play a part in the social inclusion of migrants and other people at risk of social isolation. For example, collective means of transport (e.g. vans, minibuses and people carriers) could be shared among the not-for-profit associations working with migrant people and other categories at risk of exclusion, to accompany their beneficiaries to social, health and cultural services. Finally, local authorities and city stakeholders should encourage the creation of innovative start-up and peer-to-peer services providing, low cost sharing mobility services. This would not only improve social inclusion but also positively contribute to the local economy.

Notes

1 For more information visit project's website at the url www.riderproject.eu.

2 Information available from https://dati.istat.it/Index.aspx?DataSetCode=DCIS_POPRES1.

3 Information available at: https://www.istat.it/it/files//2017/07/A-AUDIZIONE-PERIFERIE_NOTA-METODOLOGICA.pdf.

4 'Palermo Public Transportation Statistics'. Global Public Transit Index by Moovit. Retrieved June 19, 2017.

References

Andreotti, A., Anselmi, G., & Hoffmann, C. (2018). Are weak relations working? Sharing platforms and social capital. *Sociologia del Lavoro, 152,* 87–103. https://doi.org/10.3280/SL2018-152005.

Arcidiacono, D., & Pais, I. (2017). *Reciprocità, fiducia e relazioni nei servizi di mobilità condivisa: Un'analisi sul carpooling di BlaBlaCar*. Paper presented at the I Conference of SISEC Società Italiana Sociologia Economica (pp. 26–28). Genuary: Università La Sapienza Roma. Available at: https://www.sisec.it/wp-content/uploads/2017/02/Arcidiacono-Pais-Car-pooling-bla-bla-car-full-paper-SISEC.pdf.

Berry, J. M., & Wilcox, C. (2018). *The interest group society*. New York: Routledge.

Berry, J. W. (1992). Acculturation and adaptation in a new society. *International Migration, 30,* 69–85. https://doi.org/10.1111/j.1468-2435.1992.tb00776.x.

Berry, J. W. (1997). Immigration, acculturation, and adaptation. *Applied Psychology, 46,* 5–34. https://doi.org/10.1111/j.1464-0597.1997.tb01087.x.

Berry, J. W. (2005). Acculturation: Living successfully in two cultures. *International Journal of Intercultural Relations, 29,* 697–712. https://doi.org/10.1016/j.ijintrel.2005.07.013.

Berry, J. W. (2017). *Mutual intercultural relations*. Cambridge: Cambridge University Press.

Berry, J. W., & Sam, D. L. (2013). Accommodating cultural diversity and achieving equity. *European Psychologist,* 18, 151–157. https://doi.org/10.1027/1016-9040/a000167.

Berry, J. W., Poortinga, Y. H., Segall, M. H., & Dasen, P. R. (2002). *Cross-cultural psychology: Research and applications*. Cambridge: Cambridge University Press.

Bertucci, L., & Piras, V. (2018). *Osservatorio Mobilità Sostenibile in Italia. Indagine sulle principali 50 città*. Associazione Euromobility. Available at: https://www.euromobility.org/dati-osservatorio-2018/.

Bradshaw, J., Kemp, P., Baldwin, S., & Rowe, A. (2004). *The drivers of social exclusion: A review of the literature for the social exclusion unit in the breaking the cycle series*. London: Office of the Deputy Prime Minister.

Cass, N., Shove, E., & Urry, J. (2005). Social exclusion, mobility and access. *The Sociological Review, 53*(3), 539–555.

Clark, J., & Curl, A. (2016). Bicycle and car share schemes as inclusive modes of travel? A socio-spatial analysis in Glasgow. *Social Inclusion, 4,* 83–99. https://doi.org/10.17645/si.v4i3.510.

Currie, G. (Ed.). (2011). *New perspectives and methods in transport and social exclusion research*. Emerald: Bingley.

Currie, G., & Delbosc, A. (2011). *Field survey results*. In G. Currie (Ed.), *New perspectives and methods in transport and social exclusion research*. Bingley: Emerald.

Currie, G., & Stanley, J. (2008). Investigating links between social capital and public transport. *Transport Reviews, 28,* 529–547. https://doi.org/10.1080/01441640701817197.

Giacon, M. (2018). *La sharing mobility* (Master's thesis). Università Ca' Foscari Venezia, Italy. https://hdl.handle.net/10579/12289.

Hewitt-Taylor, J. (2001). Use of constant comparative analysis in qualitative research. *Nursing Standard, 15,* 39–42. https://doi.org/10.7748/ns2001.07.15.42.39.c3052.

Hiscock, R., Mudu, P., Braubach, M., Martuzzi, M., Perez, L., & Sabel, C. (2014). Wellbeing impacts of city policies for reducing greenhouse gas emissions. *International Journal of Environmental Research and Public Health, 11,* 12312–12345. https://doi.org/10.3390/ijerph111212312.

Inguglia, C., & Musso, P. (2015). Intercultural profiles and adaptation among immigrant and autochthonous adolescents. *Europe's Journal of Psychology, 11,* 79–99. https://doi.org/10.5964/ejop.v11i1.872.

Inguglia, C., Musso, P., & Lo Coco, A. (2017). Intercultural relations in Italy. In J. W. Berry (Ed.), *Mutual intercultural relations* (pp. 210–230). Cambridge: Cambridge University Press.

Jain, J., & Guiver, J. (2001). Turning the car inside out: Transport, equity and environment. *Social Policy & Administration, 35,* 569–586. https://doi.org/10.1111/1467-9515.t01-1-00254.

Jasper, M. A. (1994). Issues in phenomenology for researchers of nursing. *Journal of Advanced Nursing, 19,* 309–314. https://doi.org/10.1111/j.1365-2648.1994.tb01085.x.

Knowles, R. D. (2006). Transport shaping space: Differential collapse in time-space. *Journal of Transport Geography, 14,* 407–425.

Kodransky, M., & Lewenstein, G. (2014). *Connecting low-income people to opportunity with shared mobility.* Institute for Transportation and Development Policy. Available at: https://livingcities.s3.amazonaws.com/resource/284/download.pdf.

Krueger, R. A. (2006). Analyzing focus group interviews. *Journal of Wound Ostomy and Continence Nursing, 33,* 478–481. https://doi.org/10.1097/00152192-200609000-00004.

Levinson, D. (2010). Equity effects of road pricing: A review. *Transport Reviews, 30,* 33–57. https://doi.org/10.1080/01441640903189304.

Levitas, R., Pantazis, C., Fahmy, E., Gordon, D., Lloyd-Reichling, E., & Patsios, D. (2007). *The multi-dimensional analysis of social exclusion.* Department for Communities and Local. Available at: https://dera.ioe.ac.uk/6853/1/multidimensional.pdf.

Lodovici, L. S., & Torchio, N. (2015). *Social inclusion in EU public transport.* Brussels: Publications Office of the EU. https://doi.org/10.2861/75342.

Lucas, K. (2012). Transport and social exclusion: Where are we now? *Transport Policy, 20,* 105–113. https://doi.org/10.1016/j.tranpol.2012.01.013.

Maddrell, A., Ricci, M., Wigley, E. & Casado-Diaz, M. (2016). *Review of recent Bristol economic migrants: Needs and strategies.* Available at: https://uwe-repository.worktribe.com/output/909747/review-of-recent-bristol-economic-migrants-needs-and-strategies.

Mattioli, G. (2017). 'Forced car ownership' in the UK and Germany: Socio-spatial patterns and potential economic stress impacts. *Social Inclusion, 5,* 147–160. https://doi.org/10.17645/si.v5i4.1081.

Midgley, P. (2009). The role of smart bike-sharing systems in urban mobility. *Journeys, 2,* 23–31. Available at: https://esci-ksp.org/wp/wp-content/uploads/2012/04/The-Role-of-Smart-Bike-sharing-Systems.pdf.

Osservatorio Nazionale sulla Sharing Mobility. (2018). *Terzo Rapporto Nazionale sulla Sharing Mobility.* Fondazione per lo Sviluppo Sostenibile. Available at: https://osservatoriosharingmobility.it/wp-content/uploads/2019/07/come-sta-la-sharing-mobility_III-Rapporto-SM_13-e-FRONT.pdf.

Pacione, M. (2003). Urban environmental quality and human wellbeing: A social geographical perspective. *Landscape and Urban Planning, 65*(1–2), 19–30. https://doi.org/10.1016/S0169-2046(02)00234-7.

Parigi, P., & State, B. (2014). Disenchanting the world: The impact of technology on relationships. In L. M. Aiello, & D. McFarland (Eds.), *Social informatics. SocInfo 2014.* Lecture notes in computer science (Vol. 8851). Cham, Switzerland: Springer.

Parkhurst, G., & Seedhouse, A. (2019). Will the 'smart mobility' revolution matter? In I. Docherty, & J. Shaw (Eds.), *Transport matters.* Bristol: Policy Press.

Pereira, R. H., Schwanen, T., & Banister, D. (2017). Distributive justice and equity in transportation. *Transport Reviews, 37,* 170–191. https://doi.org/10.1080/01441647.2016.1257660.

Price, M., & Chacko, E. (2012). *Migrants' inclusion in cities: Innovative urban policies and practices.* Paper prepared for UN-Habitat and UNESCO Marie Price and Elizabeth Chacko. Available at: https://www.researchgate.net/publication/272023289_Migrants'_Inclusion_in_Cities_Innovative_Urban_Policies_and_Practices_Prepared_for_UN-Habitat_and_UNESCO_Marie_Price_and_Elizabeth_Chacko.

Pucci, P., & Colleoni, M. (Eds.). (2016). *Understanding mobilities for designing contemporary cities.* Milan: Springer.

Pucher, J., & Buehler, R. (2010). Walking and cycling for healthy cities. *Built Environment, 36*(4), 391–414.

Ricci, M. (2015). Bike sharing: A review of evidence on impacts and processes of implementation and operation. *Research in Transportation Business and Management, 15,* 28–38. https://doi.org/10.1016/j.rtbm.2015.03.003.

Ricci, M. (2016). Young age, mobility and social inclusion in a disadvantaged urban periphery in England. In L. Murray, & S. Robertson (Eds.), *Intergenerational mobilities: Relationality, age and the lifecourse*, New York: Routledge.

Ricci, M. (2017). *Days out by train in the West of England final project report*. Available at: https://uwe-repository.worktribe.com/output/886976/days-out-by-train-in-the-west-of-england-final-project-report.

Ricci, M., Parkhurst, G., & Jain, J. (2016). Transport policy and social inclusion. *Social Inclusion, 4,* 1–6. https://doi.org/10.17645/si.v4i3.668.

Schor, J. B., Fitzmaurice, C., Carfagna, L. B., Attwood-Charles, W., & Poteat, E. D. (2016). Paradoxes of openness and distinction in the sharing economy. *Poetics, 54,* 66–81. https://doi.org/10.1016/j.poetic.2015.11.001.

Schwanen, T., Lucas, K., Akyelken, N., Solsona, D. C., Carrasco, J. A., & Neutens, T. (2015). Rethinking the links between social exclusion and transport disadvantage through the lens of social capital. *Transportation Research Part A: Policy and Practice, 74,* 123–135. https://doi.org/10.1016/j.tra.2015.02.012.

Smorto, G. (2018). La tutela del contraente debole nella platform economy. *Giornale di Diritto del Lavoro e di Relazioni Industriali, 158,* 423–443. https://doi.org/10.3280/GDL2018-158008.

Social Exclusion Unit. (2003). *Making the connections: Transport and social exclusion. Final report*. London: Office of the Deputy Prime Minister. Available at: https://www.ilo.org/wcmsp5/groups/public/—ed_emp/—emp_policy/—invest/documents/publication/wcms_asist_8210.pdf.

Stanley, J., & Stanley, J. (2017). The importance of transport for social inclusion. *Social Inclusion, 5,* 108–115. https://doi.org/10.17645/si.v5i4.1289.

Urry, J. (2012). Social networks, mobile lives and social inequalities. *Journal of Transport Geography, 21,* 24–30. https://doi.org/10.1016/j.jtrangeo.2011.10.003.

Welsch, J., Conrad, K., & Wittowsky, D. (2018). Exploring immigrants travel behaviour: Empirical findings from Offenbach am Main, Germany. *Transportation, 45,* 733–750. https://doi.org/10.1007/s11116-016-9748-9.

Acceptance of Shared, Electric and Autonomous Mobility in Lisbon, Portugal

Joana Vicente, Catarina Rolim, and Patrícia Baptista

Abstract In a context where alternative services and products continue to arise mainly in urban centers to mitigate transport externalities, a very influential variable continues to be if people are willing to accept and use these new concepts. Consequently, the objective of this work was to analyze the potential consumer adoption of shared autonomous vehicles. The case study held in the Lisbon Metropolitan Area (LMA) in Portugal, considered a shared and autonomous vehicle, with an assumed cost of 7 cents/km in a 33-min trip. An average acceptance of 44% was obtained and affected by some of the considered variables. One of those variables was age, with younger people being more prone to adopt. In fact, people aged below 35 present more than 50% choice in shared, electric and autonomous vehicles, while for older groups, the percentages of choice are more distributed. People that usually drive are less prone to adopt shared and autonomous vehicles. Travel period also presents differences in alternative choice, since people that travel out of the rush-hour period are more reluctant to change. However, in order for this adoption to be successful, it is crucial to understand what makes people choose them and adopt and, for this, assessing lifestyles and behaviors plays an essential role.

Keywords Transport externalities · Electric vehicles · Shared mobility · Autonomous vehicles · User acceptance

---

Electronic supplementary material The online version of this chapter (https://doi.org/10.1007/978-3-030-57725-4_5) contains supplementary material, which is available to authorized users.

J. Vicente · C. Rolim · P. Baptista (✉)
Center for Innovation, Technology and Policy Research, Instituto Superior Técnico, Universidade de Lisboa, Lisbon, Portugal
e-mail: patricia.baptista@tecnico.ulisboa.pt

G. Smorto and I. Vinci (eds.), *The Role of Sharing Mobility in Contemporary Cities*, UNIPA Springer Series, https://doi.org/10.1007/978-3-030-57725-4_5

1 Introduction

Owning a car is intricately connected with social aspects, since it allows traveling with freedom of schedules and routes, while also guaranteeing a level of comfort and accessibility during the journey which is difficult to find in public transports. Besides, traditionally, buying a car is seen as an important step in adult life, and being able to take the car to the workplace daily is seen as a sign of social status. Consequently, people who own a car feel free and empowered, not having to depend on others to make their daily life.

In parallel, purchase power has also been increasing along time, resulting in increasing motorizations rates (vehicles per 1000 inhabitants). The EU-28 motorization rate has increased to 516 vehicles per 1000 inhabitants in 2017, in comparison with 342 in 1990 (EUROSTAT 2019a). For Portugal, motorization stands currently at 492 vehicles with an average increase of 4% per year (EUROSTAT 2019a). This increasing number of vehicles has been leading, throughout the years, to several problems easily noticeable by all commuters from drivers to pedestrians. One example is the combination of increasing traffic congestion and pressure for parking associated to the high number of vehicles, mainly visible in the major cities across Europe.

The externalities caused by transport use in the urban environment are often disregarded by the public in general but are very significant in terms of energy and environmental impacts. Transport activities were responsible for 31% of final energy consumption in the EU-28 in 2017, while for Portugal that value reached 38% (EUROSTAT 2019a). For greenhouse gases emissions (GHG), transport activities were responsible for 27% of GHG emissions in 2017 for the EU-28, with a 28% value for Portugal (EUROSTAT 2019a). The emissions of local air pollutants from the transport activities have been decreasing (from 1990 to 2017, carbon monoxide and non-methane volatile organic compounds diminished by around 87%, sulfur oxides by 66% and nitrogen oxides by 40%; reductions of 44% for PM2.5 and 35% for PM10, since 2000), but exceedances of limit values continue to be observed in urban context (EEA 2017).

Despite this increasing motorization rate, younger generations seem to care less about owning a car than the previous ones and are more disposed to live close to the city centers with easier access to public transportation and seem more disposed to use it as well, instead of driving to the workplace (Rodrigue 2017). These factors give strength to a paradigm shift in transportation, with the emergence of different market concepts, such as electrification of transports, mobility-as-a-service (MaaS), ride-sharing and autonomous vehicles.

The use of information and communication technologies (ICT) by the transport users (e.g., cell phones) and also its deployment in vehicles (e.g., sensorization of vehicles) results in an increasing connectivity of transport stakeholders. It enables the development and deployment of new concepts, from technologies to products and services. For example, connectivity with other vehicles would allow vehicles to send information between each other, not only about traffic problems, but also would let the car in the front inform the car behind if it will suddenly stop, brake or any other dangerous maneuvers. The connectivity of vehicle to the road infrastructure may also result in higher levels of vehicle automation choosing routes with less traffic, like it already happens with apps like Waze.

Vehicle automation is expected to reduce the action of the human driver, mitigating human errors, increasing safety and diminishing fatigue behind the wheel (Papadoulis et al. 2019). Another advantage is the time users gain while sitting in the car, which can allow them to perform other activities. However, security concerns may hamper the initial adoption of autonomous vehicles, since there is the possibility of being hacked, posing special hazard to human safety and leading to road accidents (Sanguino and Dominguez 2020).

Nonetheless, several studies state that in a world of autonomous vehicles, it is expected that the number of vehicles circulating would increase, since it would become a lot easier to travel (Gruel and Stanford 2016). In spite of this, traffic would be more organized not only between the vehicle and the road infrastructure but also due to the connection between different types of vehicles and infrastructures (Lyons 2018). This integration of services would enable the promotion of alternative mobility products, giving special attention to soft modes (walking and cycling) with bigger and more adequate sidewalks for people and less congested traffic lanes Macedo et al. 2017).

Nevertheless, the optimization of the use of transport products could substantially benefit from a behavioral change in terms of sharing resources. Shared vehicles are crucial in the attempt to decrease the number of vehicles that get into the city, by decreasing vehicle ownership and by increasing the occupancy rate. Both free-floating and one-way sharing schemes have led to reductions of vehicle ownership ranging from 5 to 15 cars replaced for each car added to the sharing fleet (Transport and Environment 2017). Nonetheless, studies indicate that the type of scheme can influence ownership in different ways. Free-floating schemes present a lower impact on ownership that one-way schemes (Becker et al. 2018; Namazu and Dowlatabadi 2018). Evidence indicates that environmental concerns influence the decision to use point-to-point service, with the sustainable impact of car-sharing being perceived as a positive side effect of car-sharing (Hartl et al. 2018).

Additionally, the electrification of the transport sector currently appears as a long-term bet for improving the sector's overall energy efficiency, improves air quality and noise in cities, coupled with the promotion of the incorporation of renewable energy resources. Electric vehicles sales have been increasing, and it estimated that by 2040, approximately 550 million EV will circulate around the world (IEA 2018).

These different concepts have been advancing simultaneously, and they are highly interconnected, but one of the more crucial barriers for their advance has been user behavior and their willingness to accept and adopt these innovations. The society needs to embrace the change, requiring a behavioral and social adaption to these new concepts, making people see mobility-as-a-service and not a product, that the private car may not be so much necessary as they think and that sharing the ride can be the best option not only for the city's environment but also for them (Nykvist and Whitmarsh 2008). Consequently, this work assesses the potential consumer adoption of shared and autonomous vehicles in the context of Lisbon Metropolitan Area (LMA) in Portugal.

2 Data and Methods

The methodology applied in this work is summarized in Fig. 1, starting from a case study characterization essential to develop and deploy the survey, which was later processed to extract relevant information. The case study for this work was the Lisbon Metropolitan Area (LMA) with 18 municipalities and an area of 3015 km^2, with 2.8 million inhabitants, representing 27% of the country' population.

According to the last survey on mobility, the average trip in LMA takes 24.5 min with a distance of 11 km (INE 2018). From the total trips done, 58.9% are made in a private car, and the main purpose of the trip is commuting to and from work (30.8%) (INE 2018). The intercity movements are an important part of the mobility (34.6%) being Lisbon the municipality that receives more people with 110 entrances per 100 Lisbon inhabitants (INE 2018).

2.1 Survey Development

A survey was developed in order to assess the possible acceptance of shared electric autonomous vehicles by evaluating its impacts in two main variables: travel costs and time. The survey was divided into three parts. The first one was the typical trip characterization with the objective of understanding what kind of trip the respondent makes frequently or daily. The second part was a choice activity where the respondent picked in eight possible scenarios between three different variable alternatives, and the third part was related with the socioeconomic characterization of the inquired.

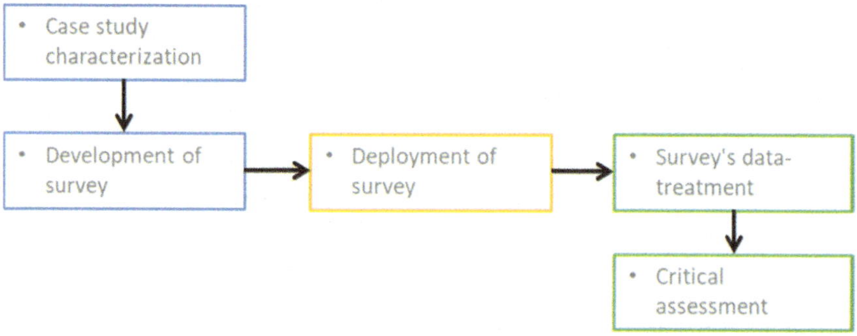

Fig. 1 Methodology layout; blue color indicates inputs for the study, yellow the sample collection stage and yellow the gathering of outputs

This survey focused on the LMA, so people had to choose the residency municipality and main destination municipality, within the 18 municipalities from LMA. The purpose of the most frequent daily trip and the transport mode used were also characterized. If a private vehicle was used, its occupancy vehicle segment and age were also inquired. For the typical trip characterization, the length and duration of trip were asked, as well as if they were performed in rush or non-rush-hour periods. The satisfaction with the transport mode used for their typical trip was also inquired, as well as the accessibility to public transports at origin and destination. The experience of respondents with alternative transport modes available in LMA was also questioned, as well as the respondent's awareness with the concept of autonomous and shared vehicles.

2.2 *Scenario Assumptions*

The response to shared and autonomous vehicles was assessed through a choice activity using eight scenarios. The scenarios were defined based on price per kilometer and travel time for each trip, but an explanatory short video was presented in order to simplify the concepts.[1] The three alternatives considered consist of:

- Conventional private gasoline car and is presented as the current solution (Alternative 1);
- Autonomous electric vehicle, called through a mobile app, picking the user up in their location and driving them to the final destination, with the user alone in the car (Alternative 2) and
- Alternative 3 which is similar to Alternative 2 except that in this option the user shares the trip with other users, which implies more stops along the trip.

The considered typical trip was of 11 km lasting 24.5 min (INE 2018). Also, based on AML mobility survey (INE 2018), the average monthly parking expenses per household are of 5.80 €, while the average monthly expense with tolls per household is of 10.60 €. For insurance and maintenance, the reference values considered are of 0.017 €/km for insurance of both types of alternatives, and for maintenance, the assumed values were of 0.063 €/km for gasoline vehicles and of 0.038 €/km for electric vehicles (Nina 2010).

2.2.1 Type of Vehicle

Regarding Alternative 1, a total cost of ownership approach was chosen, to assess the total cost and cost per kilometer (€/km). A purchase cost of 18,000 € was considered based on one of the most sold vehicles in Portugal (Mota 2018), the Renault Clio (Renault 2020). Based on the current lifetime of vehicles in Portugal (12.7 years) (ACAP 2018) and on the total kilometers traveled statistics (Pereira et al. 2019), it is possible to compute that a vehicle is estimated to drive for around 131 thousand km in its lifetime. Considering this, the total cost of parking will be of 887 €, and the total costs with tolls will be of 1609 €.

In Alternatives 2 and 3, the vehicle considered is the same, an electric autonomous vehicle that takes the users from the place most convenient to them to the final destination chose by them. This option would allow a first to last kilometer cover without the need to drive and park the car, but with freedom of movement similar to owning and driving a car. The chosen car was a Model 3 T with long range capacity, costing around 66,000 € (Tesla 2020). This car has battery capacity of 75 kWh that lasts 8 years (Verbrugge and Wampler 2017) with a taxi-like utilization of 65,000 km/year according to Lisbon usage patterns (Castel-Branco 2015), which will represent 520,000 km during the lifetime of the vehicle. However, some differences in the use of Alternatives 2 and 3 will affect the kilometers driven and its utilization cost. The considered energy consumption for a Model 3 T is of 0.20 kWh/km (EV-Database 2020). These vehicles are assumed to be owned by a company or by the state, and parking and toll costs are not directly paid by the users. In spite of that, these costs should be accounted for the final price. In this step, some hypotheses were admitted. A reduction of 50% of parking costs and an increase of 100% of tolls costs were assumed based on the fact that the vehicles would spend less time parked and would circulate more, so it is assumed that they will cross tolls more often. This translates into a cost of 443 € for parking and 3219 € for tolls.

For insurance and maintenance, the method is the same as in Alternative 1, considering the total 520,000 km in the vehicle's lifetime and the values considered for electric vehicles (Nina 2010). The insurance for BEV is the same as for an ICEV (0.017 €/km), and for maintenance, the price is of 0.038 €/km (Nina 2010). Considering these values, the total cost for insurance for 520,000 km is of 8840 €, and for maintenance, it reaches 19,760 €.

Furthermore, both for Alternatives 2 and 3, it was considered that the vehicles would work for a maximum of 12 h per day, which complies with limitations imposed by Uber (2020). However, even if these cases have no driver and no problems associated to drivers' fatigue can be taken into account, there may be recharging requirements since the vehicle will have peaks of activity during rush hours (8–10 h 17–19 h), justifying the 12 h shifts.

For the electricity costs, a 0.15 €/kWh price was considered (EUROSTAT 2019b), which combined with the vehicle's energy consumption of 0.2 kWh/km, provides a total final cost of 15,600 €. For an average speed of 27 km/h (INE 2018), during a 12 h shift, the daily total kilometers should be of 324 km, corresponding to a daily energy consumption of 64.8 kWh. This daily consumption should not require an additional recharge, since 64.8 kWh represents 86% of the total battery capacity.

2.2.2 Total Trip Time

The total travel time for Alternative 2 is assumed to be 29 min considering the 25 min on the average trip. Since there will be no need to park, a parking time of 2 min was considered (Khattak and Polak 1993) and subtracted to the 25 min time, since it is the most comparable study for the Lisbon reality, in spite of other studies that consider waiting times of up to 6 min (Rayle et al. 2016).

As for Alternative 3, the main calculations are already presented for Alternative 2, since the vehicle is the same. However, since in Alternative 3, the vehicle will have more stops because of sharing the trip, a reduction in average speed to 20 km/h was assumed. In a 12 h shift, the vehicle would then drive 240 km, which means a daily consumption of 48 kWh, representing only 64% of all battery capacity. Also, it was considered that a vehicle is occupied with at least one user only 80% of the time, the reasons for empty driving are the same as in Alternative 2, but in this case, the car will be empty for less kilometers since several users can be in the car at same time. The 80% rate of occupancy means a total of kilometers with passengers of 192 km, which corresponds to 17 trips. In Alternative 3, each trip can take up to four users representing a total of 69 passengers per day.

2.2.3 Trip Cost

Considering that gasoline cost of 0.12 €/km (Silva 2018), the total fuel cost is obtained representing a total cost of 15,745 €. The total cost of insurance and maintenance is also calculated based on a €/km factor (0.017 €/km for insurance and 0.063 €/km for maintenance (Nina 2010), resulting in 2231 € and 8266 €, respectively. Including purchase, fuel insurance and maintenance costs, the total cost of ownership goes to 46,738 € for Alternative 1 corresponding to 0.356 €/km supported by the user.

Regarding Alternative 2, other assumptions had to be defined. It was considered that the vehicle was occupied only 60% of the time, since it only takes one request at a time and it has to go empty from dropping point to the location of next user, which should be the closest request possible. This translates into 194.4 km driven with a passenger on board per day, and considering an average trip of 11 km, this translates to 17 full trips. Since one trip takes only one user, this represents 17 users per day. This information is not needed for the following calculations, since 194.4 km already accounts the number of trips. Accounting all the cost components presented, the total cost obtained is of 112 k€, while the cost per km reaches 0.216 €/km. Additionally, based on information from platforms like Uber, a 25% share of total cost allocated to the company (Soyinka 2019) was defined, resulting in a final price is of 0.270 €/km. This cost is supported only by one user and considers the whole vehicle's lifetime (520,000 km).

Considering the prices calculated previously, the total cost will be the same as in Alternative 2, however now is necessary to consider that the trip is divided with up to four other users. The cost per kilometer (0.216 €/km) is then divided by the four users per trip with a final result of around 6 cents/km. Using as base the 25% profit of Alternative 2, it was considered that in Alternative 3, the profit should be 35% since the occupancy is higher, resulting in a 0.073 €/km final cost per user. Once again, this cost considers a lifetime of 520,000 km with each trip divided by four people.

Table 1 Table presented on the survey, corresponding to the calculated scenario

	Conventional private vehicle	Autonomous electric vehicle (car-sharing)	Autonomous electric vehicle (ride-sharing)
	Alternative 1	Alternative 2	Alternative 3
Trip cost (€/km)	0.36	0.27	0.07
Total trip time (min)	25	29	33

The total travel time for Alternative 3 is of 33 min, considering the 25 min average trip, the 2 min parking time and 10 min of waiting time, assuming it would have more stops than the previous alternative (Krueger et al. 2016). Table 1 summarizes the previous cost and time calculations. This table was presented as one of the scenarios in the online survey, considered the business-as-usual (BAU) scenario.

2.3 *Scenario Definition, Survey Deployment and Data Processing*

The following step was to define an interval in which the price and times could variate. A price interval 20% below and 20% above the calculated value was chosen, in order to differentiate prices (see Table 2). To help narrow down the number of possible scenarios, the lowest price for conventional private vehicle was discarded (red value in Table 2), considering this vehicle shall get costlier, due to improvements on several car components or even considering possible taxes to apply to purchasing a vehicle. For autonomous electric alternatives, the highest prices attributed were also discarded since the technology should tend to become cheaper (red values in Table 2).

The same assumption was made for time intervals, in which, the fastest time for Alternative 1 was discarded, since as mentioned before, the volume of traffic has been increasing throughout time, and slower trips in autonomous electric vehicles were removed, since with more of these vehicles on the streets, the waiting times can decrease (red values in Table 3). For this time assumption, a 4 min difference was considered, as presented in Table 3, which makes the real-time coincide with the worst time of the previous alternative.

With six possible prices and six possible trip times, there were still 64 possible scenarios to construct. According to the literature (Sanko 2001), in stated preferences

Table 2 Price variations, in bold, are the BAU values and in red are the disregarded values

	Alternative 1	Alternative 2	Alternative 3
−20%	0.28	0.22	0.06
Calculated price	**0.36**	**0.27**	**0.07**
+20%	0.43	0.33	0.09

Table 3 Time variations, in bold, are the BAU values and in red are the disregarded values

	Alternative 1	Alternative 2	Alternative 3
−4 min	21	25	29
Calculated time	**25**	**29**	**33**
+4 min	29	33	37

activities, people only respond carefully until 5–9 scenarios. As a result, the most interesting and relevant ones were chosen to be displayed. Table 4 presents all the scenarios presented in the survey. The first scenario presents the values of the BAU situation. The following seven scenarios are combinations of all the six possible times and prices. For the majority of the tables, price and time correspond to the best or worst options for each alternative, except for scenario 4 where is combined the longest (worst) time with the lowest (best) price and scenario 7 that is the reverse, meaning, the shortest times with highest prices.

The survey was available online from July to August 2019 obtaining 354 answers from which 250 were complete, valid and analyzed.

Microsoft Excel and SPSS were used to process the survey results. Excel was used to understand how the variables affect each other, which were the main preferences and understand the respondent profile and daily trip, whereas SPSS was used to test the statistic relevance of some of the variables.

Table 4 Scenarios presented in the survey

		Conventional private vehicle	Autonomous electric vehicles (car-sharing)	Autonomous electric vehicle (ride-sharing)
		Alternative 1	Alternative 2	Alternative 3
1	Trip cost (€/km)	0.36	0.27	0.07
	Total trip time (min)	25	29	33
2	Trip cost (€/km)	0.43	0.27	0.06
	Total trip time (min)	29	29	29
3	Trip cost (€/km)	0.36	0.22	0.07
	Total trip time (min)	25	25	33
4	Trip cost (€/km)	0.36	0.22	0.06
	Total trip time (min)	29	29	33
5	Trip cost (€/km)	0.36	0.27	0.06
	Total trip time (min)	25	29	29
6	Trip cost (€/km)	0.43	0.22	0.06
	Total trip time (min)	29	25	29
7	Trip cost (€/km)	0.43	0.27	0.07
	Total trip time (min)	25	25	29
8	Trip cost (€/km)	0.43	0.22	0.07
	Total trip time (min)	29	25	33

To know which test to use, it is necessary to evaluate if the data is parametric, by testing the normality and variance homogeneity of the distribution. The normality is, in this situation, analyzed with Shapiro–Wilk test since the sample has a size (N) superior to 100. The distribution is normal if the p-value is higher than 0.05 ($p > 0.05$), since the null hypothesis (H0) that the distribution is normal. For variance homogeneity, the test used is the Levene's test where the distribution varies homogeneously if $p > 0.05$, since H0 is that the variances are equal (Field 2009).

For the data to be parametric, the distribution must be normal, homogeneously variated, and the data must be distributed in intervals and independent. In the cases where all the needs are met, the test T-Student is usually applied. When the data is not parametric, the tests applied are the nonparametric ones. The nonparametric tests to be used are Mann–Whitney test when the grouping variable only divides in two different groups and Kruskal–Wallis when the grouping variables have more than two groups (Field 2009). Three variables are satisfaction and accessibility rates. In these cases, since the data is nonparametric, the test used is a Spearman correlation.

After running normality and homogeneity tests, statistical significance was then analyzed. For all the significative variables reported below, it was seen that none of them were distributed normally except for age of the vehicle for those who prefer not answer the household' income question and for satisfaction in those who travel in a private vehicle as a passenger. For the first, SPSS was not capable of running Levene's test, but these respondents correspond only to 4% of the sample. For the last, Levene's test showed that the variance is homogeneous with $p > 0.05$, but again, these respondents correspond only to 6% of the sample. Therefore, both of the mentioned groups were considered not meaningful for the analysis regarding household income and satisfaction, respectively. With these results, it is fair to use nonparametric tests.

Focusing now on the nonparametric tests, for all the variables that were affected by the other variable, the test used was Kruskal–Wallis except for the variables of new mobility alternatives grouped by acquaintance of autonomous vehicle that have a binary answer (yes or no). After that, to understand between which groups reside the difference, the Post-Hoc Bonferroni corrections were run.

3 Results and Discussion

3.1 Demographic Characterization

The main demographic characterization of the sample is presented in Table 5. The respondent's distribution in terms of gender was of 54.4% of women and 45.6% of men, with a concentration of younger (30% below 25) and adult and senior people (59.2% above 35). Most of the respondents finished education in secondary school (35.2%) or bachelor (40.3%). The sample may be a bit skewed since the survey was firstly deployed in students' groups with 24.5% of student responses. When inquired about household income, 60.3% of the respondents state that their household income

Table 5 Demographic characterization (%)

Variable	Level	Average	Inter-municipal	Intra-municipal
Gender	Female	54.4	55.1	53.2
	Male	45.6	44.9	46.8
Age	<18	1.6	0.6	3.2
	18–25	28.4	27.6	29.8
	26–35	10.8	10.3	11.7
	36–50	28.0	30.8	23.4
	51–65	29.2	20.1	27.7
	>65	2.00	0.6	4.3
Education	Basic education	0.8	–	2.1
	Secondary education	35.2	35.3	35.1
	Bachelor	40.4	40.4	40.4
	Masters	19.6	23.1	13.8
	Ph.D.	2.0	–	5.32
	Other	2.0	–	3.2
Work situation	Unemployed	2.8	4.5	–
	Employed	62.4	66.7	55.3
	Student	24.8	19.2	34.0
	Retired	5.6	3.9	5.3
	Other	4.4		5.3
Drivers' license	Yes	91.8	94.2	89.4
	No	8.2	5.8	10.6
Number of people in household	1	8.4	7.1	10.6
	2	23.2	21.2	26.6
	3	26.4	32.1	17.0
	4	35.2	32.1	40.4
	5	6.4	7.7	4.3
	6 or more	0.4		1.0
Income	My household income allows me to live with struggle	2.8	3.9	1.0
	My household income allows me to live with moderation	60.4	60.3	60.6
	My household income allows me to live with ease	29.6	30.1	28.7
	Rather not answer	7.2	5.7	9.6

allows them to live moderately and 30.1% stated to live with ease. These results are similar to the ones presented in the AML mobility survey (INE 2018).

3.2 Trip Characterization

Regarding the typical trip performed daily, the survey results showed 62.4% of trips occur between municipalities, while 37.6% of trips occur inside each municipality. The processing of answers regarding trip duration and length enables the characterization of trip variables, as presented in Table 6. The typical trip has 19 km and takes 31 min, with an average speed of 36 km/h. Looking into the disaggregation between inter and intra-municipality commutes, for inter-municipality trips alone, the traveling time increases to 38 min and 24 km with an average speed of 39 km/h, and for intra-municipality movements, they have an average time of 20 min, distance of 10 km and an average speed of 31 km/h.

Focusing on transport mode, trips done in private car alone last mainly between 10 and 30 min, representing 54.5% of the trips done as a driver and 40.0% of the trips done as a passenger, as seen in Table 7. Also, the trips done by public transportation have mainly a duration between 30 and 60 min (51.4%).

On the choice of transport mode, 18.4% of the respondents are young people, with ages below 25 that take public transportation showing a preference of the group for public transports, while older people prefer private vehicles with 48.8% out of

Table 6 Duration, distance and speed summarized according to inter or intra-municipal trip and the average

	Inter-municipality	Intra-municipality	Average
Time (min)	37.5	19.8	30.8
Distance (km)	24.0	10.4	18.9
Speed (km/h)	38.8	31.5	36.1

Table 7 Transport mode distribution by duration in all trips

Transport mode	10 min or less (%)	Between 10 and 30 min (%)	Between 30 and 60 min (%)	More than 60 min (%)
Walk or bicycle	60.0	33.3	0.0	6.7
Public transport	1.4	24.3	51.4	23.0
Private vehicle as a driver	17.9	54.5	23.4	4.1
Private vehicle as a passenger	20.0	40.0	33.3	6.7
Shared vehicle	0.0	100.0	0.0	0.0
Total	15.6	43.6	30.8	10.0

58.0% belonging to the three last age groups, as seen in Table 8. The application of a Kruskal–Wallis test confirms that age influenced the choice of transport mode used, as showed in Table SM1 of supplementary material, which is expectable since younger people do not drive daily to school or university, being private vehicle a transport option preferred by older people.

Table 9 shows the distribution of trip duration by transport mode on a scale of satisfaction from 1 to 5, where 1 means very unsatisfied and 5 means very satisfied. The respondents that usually commute mainly by foot or bicycle are majorly satisfied with their trip, with a total of 86.7%, as seen in Table 9. Respondents that travel in their private vehicle or public transportation show a decrease in satisfaction along with an increase on travel time. However, for the same duration of trip, public transport users are always less satisfied than private vehicle users. When looking separately, people that commute by public transports are less satisfied with trips between 10 min to one hour when their daily trip is inside the same municipality, while people that travel in their private vehicle are more satisfied.

In Table 10, with the objective of relating satisfaction with transport mode and trip duration, a Spearman correlation was run. Since significance is below 0.05, the variables are considered to be correlated, which means that the transport mode and trip duration have influence on the level of satisfaction with the daily trip.

To relate accessibility to public transportation with chosen transport mode, a Spearman correlation was run, as presented in Table 11. For inter-municipal trips, it can be seen that the transport mode is correlated only with accessibility in the destination, while for intra-municipal trips, it is correlated with both accessibilities but more with destination accessibility to public transport.

It is interesting to notice that for all the public transport accessibility satisfaction level (from 1 for low accessibility to public transport to 5 for high accessibility),

Table 8 Transport mode preference distribution by age

Transport mode	Less than 18 years (%)	18–25 years (%)	26–35 years (%)	36–50 years (%)	51–65 years (%)	More than 65 years (%)
Walk or bicycle	0.0	3.6	1.2	0.8	0.0	0.4
Public transport	0.4	18.0	5.2	2.8	3.2	0.0
Private vehicle as a driver	0.0	4.8	4.4	22.4	24.8	1.6
Private vehicle as a passenger	1.2	2.0	0.0	1.6	1.2	0.0
Shared vehicle	0.0	0.0	0.0	0.4	0.0	0.0
Total	1.6	28.4	10.8	28.0	29.2	2.0

Table 9 Satisfaction with daily trip by transport mode and duration

Scale of satisfaction	1 (%)	2 (%)	3 (%)	4 (%)	5 (%)	Total (%)
Walk or bicycle	0.0	0.4	0.4	2.8	2.4	6.0
Less than 10 min	0.0	0.0	0.0	1.6	2.0	3.6
10–30 min	0.0	0.4	0.4	1.2	0.0	2.0
More than 60 min	0.0	0.0	0.0	0.0	0.4	0.4
Public transport	1.6	6.8	14.4	6.8	0.0	29.6
Less than 10 min	0.0	0.0	0.4	0.0	0.0	0.4
10–30 min	0.4	0.8	3.6	2.4	0.0	7.2
30–60 min	0.0	2.8	9.2	3.2	0.0	15.2
More than 60 min	1.2	3.2	1.2	1.2	0.0	6.8
Private vehicle as a driver	1.2	2.4	18.0	24.4	12.0	58.0
Less than 10 min	0.0	0.0	2.4	2.8	5.2	10.4
10–30 min	0.0	1.2	11.2	14.0	5.2	31.6
30–60 min	0.8	0.8	3.6	7.2	1.2	13.6
More than 60 min	0.4	0.4	0.8	0.4	0.4	2.4

Table 10 Spearman correlation between satisfaction with duration and transport mode (significant variables in bold)

Correlations—Spearman's rho				
Inter-municipal		Satisfaction	Duration	Transport mode
Satisfaction	Correlation coefficient	1.000	−0.365	−0.339
	Sig	–	**0.000**	**0.000**
	N	156	156	156
Duration	Correlation coefficient	−0.365	1.000	0.448
	Sig. two-tailed	**0.000**		**0.000**
	N	156	156	156
Transport mode	Correlation coefficient	−0.339	0.448	1.000
	Sig. two-tailed	**0.000**	**0.000**	–
	N	156	156	156
Intra-municipal		Satisfaction	Duration	Transport mode
Satisfaction	Correlation coefficient	1.000	−0.448	−0.192
	Sig. two-tailed	–	**0.000**	0.063
	N	94	94	94
Duration	Correlation coefficient	−0.448	1.000	0.121
	Sig. two-tailed	**0.000**	–	0.245
	N	94	94	94
Transport mode	Correlation coefficient	−0.192	0.121	1.000
	Sig. two-tailed	0.063	0.245	–
	N	94	94	94

Table 11 Spearman correlation between public transport accessibilities and transport mode (significant variables in bold)

Correlations—Spearman's rho				
Inter-municipal		At residence	On the destination	Transport mode
At residence	Correlation coefficient	1.000	0.317	0.136
	Sig	–	**0.000**	0.093
	N	154	151	154
On the destination	Correlation coefficient	0.317	1.000	0.364
	Sig. two-tailed	**0.000**	–	**0.000**
	N	151	153	153
Transport mode	Correlation coefficient	0.136	0.364	1.000
	Sig. two-tailed	0.093	**0.000**	–
	N	154	153	156
Intra-municipal		At residence	On the destination	Transport mode
At residence	Correlation coefficient	1.000	0.686	0.205
	Sig. two-tailed	–	**0.000**	**0.047**
	N	94	93	94
On the destination	Correlation coefficient	0.686	1.000	0.383
	Sig. two-tailed	**0.000**	–	**0.000**
	N	93	93	93
Transport mode	Correlation coefficient	0.205	0.383	1.000
	Sig. two-tailed	**0.047**	**0.000**	–
	N	94	93	94

most of the respondents attributed the same evaluation for accessibility in the area of residence and of their workplace. Furthermore, people that move between municipalities declare to have worse accessibility both in their residence and destination municipalities with about the double of people declaring accessibilities of 1 or 2. Another interesting fact is that even with better accessibilities (4 or 5), some of the supposed public transport trips are replaced with walking or biking.

Figure 2 summarizes the most significant variables that influence transport choice and consequent impacts. In general, users prefer driving their vehicle than using public transport, with age and accessibility to transports being important variables in this transport choice. Most of these trips occur in rush hours and have a considerable trip duration.

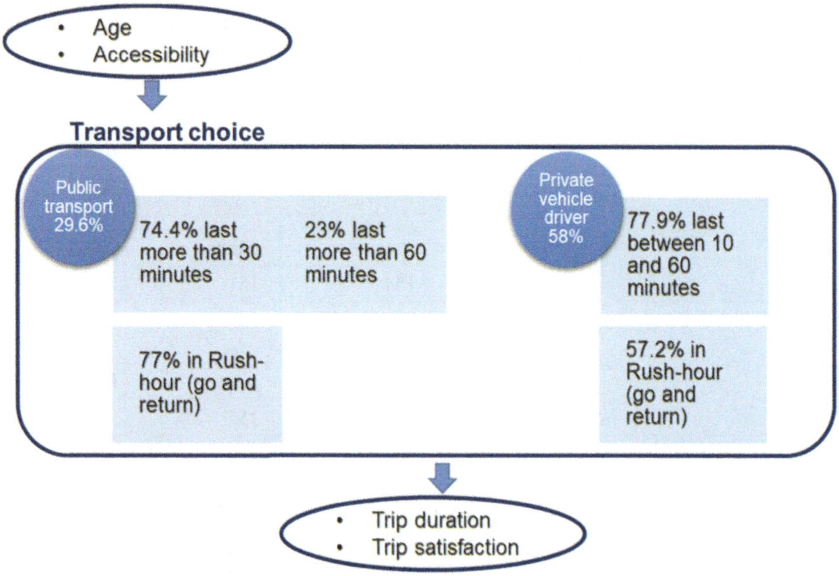

Fig. 2 Summary of trip characterization findings

3.3 Acceptance of Autonomous and Shared Mobility

Table 12 presents the distribution between alternative choices in each scenario. Alternative 3 is always the most frequently chosen. The table where Alternative 3 is less chosen is Table 3, with a percentage of 39.2%, probably because Table 3 presented the worst time and price for Alternative 3, while Alternatives 1 and 2 presented the best possible time and prices. While the scenario that presents the highest percentage of choice on Alternative 3 is scenario 5 (the best time and price) when compared with Alternative 2 (worst time and price).

Table 12 Alternative choice distribution

Table	Alternative 1 (%)	Alternative 2 (%)	Alternative 3 (%)
1	30.8	28.4	40.8
2	22.8	31.2	46.0
3	25.2	35.6	39.2
4	23.2	33.2	43.6
5	23.6	28.8	47.6
6	20.0	36.0	44.0
7	19.6	34.0	46.4
8	19.6	36.4	44.0
Average	23.0	33.0	44.0

Table 13 Alternative choice distribution by age

Age	Alternative 1 (%)	Alternative 2	Alternative 3
Less than 18 years	12.5	50.0	37.5
18–25 years	9.3	33.8	56.9
26–35 years	17.6	29.6	52.8
36–50 years	27.9	35.2	37.0
51–65 years	34.8	29.5	35.8
More than 65 years	20.0	45.0	35.0
Total	23.1	33.0	44.0

Table 13 presents an average of percentage of choice in the eight tables presented to the respondents and portraits the influence of age. Younger groups prefer Alternative 3 more clearly than older groups, for which percentages between each alternative are more similar (Fig. 3). Furthermore, the Kruskal–Wallis test was used to compare age groups, showing the existence of significant differences (*p*-value bellow 0.05) in all the alternative choice scenarios, as seen in Table SM2.

In Table 14, to facilitate the comprehension of how groups differ in alternative choice, the average for the eight tables is presented. Respondents using public transport and private vehicle as a driver present in fact very different distributions. Drivers are likely more resistant to change their behavior since they would have to trade privacy and the comfort they are used to in their trip (Fig. 3). These differences regarding the transport mode were shown to be significant, as can be seen in Table SM3.

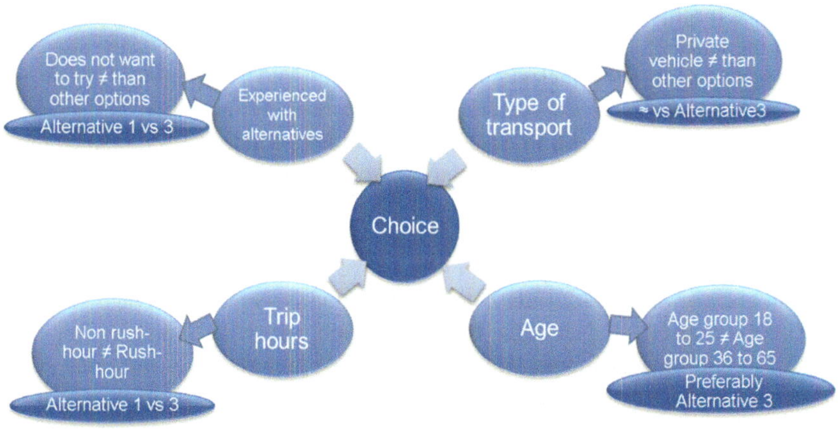

Fig. 3 Summary of acceptance of autonomous and shared mobility

Table 14 Alternative choice distribution by transport mode

Transport mode	Alternative 1 (%)	Alternative 2	Alternative 3
Walk or bicycle	2.5	38.3	59.2
Public transport	14.2	31.8	54.1
Private vehicle as a driver	31.8	32.2	36.0
Private vehicle as a passenger	5.0	42.5	52.5
Total	23.2	33.0	43.8

Table 15 Alternative choice distribution by travel in rush-hour periods

Rush-hour travel	Alternative 1 (%)	Alternative 2	Alternative 3
No	39.7	33.6	26.7
Yes, in the morning	19.7	28.5	51.8
Yes, in the afternoon	17.8	25.1	57.0
Yes, in both periods	21.4	35.0	43.6
Total	23.3	32.9	43.8

Table 15 presents the average distribution of choice between alternatives according to travel period, showing that Alternative 3 is mainly chosen by those who commute in at least one rush-hour period (Fig. 3). Traveling in rush hour or at another time period has shown to be influential in the acceptance of shared and autonomous mobility, as shown in the Kruskal–Wallis test presented in Table SM4. Rush-hour trips are marked by intense traffic and overcrowded public transportation, justifying higher acceptance for this solution.

The influence of having tried existing shared alternative services on the choice of shared and autonomous vehicles as also assessed (Fig. 3). The experience with shared vehicles, bicycles, scooters or motorcycles already available in Lisbon influences the alternative choice, as shown in the Kruskal–Wallis test in Table SM5, since those who refuse to try present a different behavior from the ones already using these types of shared services.

Nonetheless, while looking at the results as a whole, the distribution in alternatives choices is similar for every table, with Alternative 3 being the most preferred choice with an average of 44.0%, while Alternatives 1 and 2 scored an average of 23.0% and 33.0%, respectively (see Table 16). If the results are analyzed disjoined in intra-municipal and inter-municipal trips, the pattern of preferences is the same, since in intra-municipal trips, Alternatives 1 and 3 are chosen more often than in inter-municipal trips, while Alternative 2 is chosen less often.

Table 16 Alternative choice for each table and average

Table	Modality	Alternative 1 (%)	Alternative 2 (%)	Alternative 3 (%)
1	Inter-municipal	30.1	30.8	39.1
	Intra-municipal	31.9	24.5	43.6
	Total	30.8	28.4	40.8
2	Inter-municipal	21.8	33.3	44.9
	Intra-municipal	24.5	27.7	47.9
	Total	22.8	31.2	46.0
3	Inter-municipal	25.0	38.5	36.5
	Intra-municipal	25.5	30.9	43.6
	Total	25.2	35.6	39.2
4	Inter-municipal	21.8	35.9	42.3
	Intra-municipal	25.5	28.7	45.7
	Total	23.2	33.2	43.6
5	Inter-municipal	22.4	31.4	46.2
	Intra-municipal	25.5	24.5	50.0
	Total	23.6	28.8	47.6
6	Inter-municipal	19.9	36.5	43.6
	Intra-municipal	20.2	35.1	44.7
	Total	20.0	36.0	44.0
7	Inter-municipal	19.2	35.9	44.9
	Intra-municipal	20.2	30.9	48.9
	Total	19.6	34.0	46.4
8	Inter-municipal	18.6	38.5	42.9
	Intra-municipal	21.3	33.0	45.7
	Total	19.6	36.4	44.0
Average	Inter-municipal	22.4	35.1	42.5
	Intra-municipal	24.3	29.4	46.3
	Total	23.0	33.0	44.0

Figure 3 presents a summary of results regarding the choice of alternatives and main variables that potentially indicate who will be most willing to adopt a shared electric autonomous vehicle: public transport users, younger citizens, those who have already tried other shared and electric schemes and rush-hour commuting. In all the previous analysis, it is seen that most of the choices fell on Alternative 3, as presented in Fig. 3. This may be justified by the fact that people are becoming more and more aware of the environmental problems the world and the society are facing. Besides the environmental concerns, people that spent a lot of time in the traffic may be seen an improvement in their quality of life due to new mobility alternatives, especially Alternative 3 that has the potential to decrease more the number of vehicles in circulation, at least when compared with Alternative 2. Independently of the reason that makes people choose Alternative 3, it is an important statement that the majority would not mind sharing the vehicle with strangers. However, it should be taken into account that these conclusions result from a stated preferences experience. Stated preferences are usually more flexible, and when responding to stated preferences experience, people do not have to pay for real for the technology.

4 Conclusions

The objective of this work was to analyze the potential consumer adoption of shared autonomous vehicles. Some progress has been made on the adaption of cities to alternative mobility technologies (e.g., electric vehicles, car and bike sharing services, etc.). Furthermore, some pilot demonstrations of autonomous vehicles are already available in some cities. However, to adopt autonomous vehicles as a common car or shuttle, common legislation between countries must be prepared and set in place. Also, the user must be also prone to adopt such changes.

The case study held in AML, Portugal, considered a shared and autonomous vehicle, with an assumed cost of 7 cents/km in a 33 min trip. An average acceptance of 44% was obtained and affected by some of the considered variables. One of those variables was age, with younger people being more prone to adopt. In fact, people aged below 35 present more than 50% choice in Alternative 3, while for older groups, the percentages of choice are more distributed. People that usually drive are less prone to adopt shared and autonomous vehicles, since in average, drivers are divided between the three alternatives presenting an average of 36.0% of choice in Alternative 3, while all the other groups present a percentage of choice above 50%. Travel period also presents differences in alternative choice, since people that travel out of the rush-hour period are more reluctant to change, with only 26.2% of the non-rush-hour commuter choice. Another aspect that has showed to affect the choice is the previous experience with shared mobility alternatives already available, with those who state that would not like to try showing a clear preference for keeping on using the current alternatives. The differences between intra- and inter-municipal commuting were not considered meaningful. Despite not being a well-defined profile, it is possible to admit that the early adopters are people aged between 18 and 35 years old, which agrees with the fact that students may be an important early adopter group. Besides, rush-hour commuters are also seen as early adopters.

To improve the acceptance of these new mobility solutions, the transport system and policies should converge toward an easy adoption. Another important step is disseminating the positive impacts of these alternatives, making them easier to use and available for everybody. Addressing safety concerns is also an important step toward the promotion of adoption. In the, nowadays, ever-evolving culture of transforming cities into becoming more sustainable, citizens are continually faced with new services and solutions presented as life changing if adopted. However, in order for this adoption to be successful, it is crucial to understand what makes people choose them and adopt, and for this, assessing lifestyles and behaviors plays an essential role. In the case of shared autonomous vehicles, further work is needed addressing citizens' willingness to accept and, consequently, adopt such schemes, in order to better perceive how and who would use such a service.

Notes

1 https://www.youtube.com/watch?v=KaD03eiZONg.

Acknowledgements The authors acknowledge Fundação para a Ciência e Tecnologia for IN+ Strategic Project UID/EEA/50009/2019 and for contract CEECIND/02589/2017. This work is supported by European Union's Horizon 2020 research and innovation program under Grant Agreement No. 691895 SHAR-LLM ("Sharing Cities").

References

ACAP—Associacao Automovel de Portugal. (2018). *Estatísticas do sector automóvel edição*. Available at: https://www.velocidades.pt/wp-content/uploads/2018/09/ESTATÍSTICAS-DO-SECTOR-AUTOMÓVEL-2018.pdf.

Becker, H., Ciari, F., & Axhausen, K. W. (2018). Measuring the car ownership impact of free-floating car-sharing a case study in Basel, Switzerland. *Transportation Research Part D: Transport and Environment, 65,* 51–62.

Castel-Branco, A. P., Ribau, J. P., & Silva, C. M. (2015). Taxi fleet renewal in cities with improved hybrid powertrains: Life cycle and sensitivity analysis in Lisbon case study. *Energies, 8*(9), 1–32.

EEA—European Environment Agency. (2017). *European Union emission inventory report 1990–2015 under the UNECE convention on long-range transboundary air pollution* (p. 9).

EUROSTAT. (2019a). *Statistical pocketbook 2019. Mobility and transport*. Available at: https://ec.europa.eu/transport/facts-fundings/statistics/pocketbook-2019_en. Accessed: January 21, 2020.

EUROSTAT. (2019b). *Electricity price statistics. Statistics explained*. Available at: https://ec.europa.eu/eurostat/statistics-explained/index.php/Electricity_price_statistics.

EV-Database. (2020). *Compare hybrid and electric vehicle*. Available at: https://ev-database.org/. Accessed: January 30, 2020.

Field, A. (2009). *Discovering statistics using SPSS*. London: Sage.

Gruel, W., & Stanford, J. M. (2016). Assessing the long-term effects of autonomous vehicles: A speculative approach. *Transportation Research Procedia, 13,* 18–29.

Hartl, B., Sabitzer, T., Hofmann, E., & Penz, E. (2018). Sustainability is a nice bonus' the role of sustainability in carsharing from a consumer perspective. *Journal of Cleaner Production, 202,* 88–100.

IEA—International Energy Agency. (2018). *Global EV outlook 2018*. Available at: https://www.iea.org/reports/global-ev-outlook-2018.

INE—Instituto Nacional de Estatistica. (2018). *Inquérito à Mobilidade nas Áreas Metropolitanas do Porto e de Lisboa*. Available at: https://www.ine.pt/xportal/xmain?xpid=INE&xpgid=ine_destaques&DESTAQUESdest_boui=334619442&DESTAQUESmodo=2&xlang=pt. Accessed: January 30, 2020.

Khattak, A. Polak, J. (1993). Effect of parking information on travelers 'knowledge and behavior. *Transportation*, 373–393.

Krueger, R., Rashidi, T. H., & Rose, J. M. (2016). Preferences for shared autonomous vehicles. *Transportation Research Part C, 69,* 343–355.

Lyons, G. (2018). Getting smart about urban mobility—Aligning the paradigms of smart and sustainable. *Transportation Research Part A Policy and Practice, 115,* 4–14.
Macedo, J., Rodrigues, F., & Tavares, F. (2017). Urban sustainability mobility assessment: Indicators proposal. *Energy Procedia, 134,* 731–740.
Mota, E. (2018). CO_2: Comparação das emissões indiretas dos carros elétricos com os de combustão. *Pplware.* Available at: https://pplware.sapo.pt/motores/carros-eletricos-vs-combustao-em-emissoes-de-co2/.
Namazu, M., & Dowlatabadi, H. (2018). Vehicle ownership reduction: A comparison of one-way and two-way carsharing systems. *Transport Policy, 64,* 38–50.
Nina, M. (2010). *Introduction of electric vehicles in portugal. A cost-benefit analysis.* Dissertação para obtenção do Grau de Mestre em Engenharia Mecânica, Universidade Tecnica de Lisboa.
Nykvist, B., & Whitmarsh, L. (2008). A multi-level analysis of sustainable mobility transitions: Niche development in the UK and Sweden. *Technological Forecasting and Social Change, 75*(9), 1373–1387.
Papadoulis, A., Quddus, M., & Imprialou, M. (2019). Evaluating the safety impact of connected and autonomous vehicles on motorways. *Accident Analysis and Prevention, 124,* 12–22.
Pereira, T. C., Amaro, A., Borges, M., Silva, R., Pina, A., & Canaveira, P. (2019). *Portuguese national inventory report on greenhouse gases.* Submitted under the United Nations framework convention on climate change and the Kyoto.
Rayle, L., Dai, D., Chan, N., Cervero, R., & Shaheen, S. (2016). Just a better taxi? A survey-based comparison of taxis, transit and ridesourcing services in San Francisco. *Transport Policy, 45,* 168–178.
Renault. (2020). *Renault Portugal—Compra de veículos novos. Site oficial.* Available: https://www.renault.pt/. Accessed: January 30, 2020.
Rodrigue, J. P. (2017). *The geography of transport systems.* London, New York: Routledge.
Sanguino, P. B. T., & Dominguez, J. (2020). Review on security issues for connected autonomous vehicles. Towards cybersecurity auditing & certification of automotive industry. In *Policy implications of autonomous vehicles.* Elsevier
Sanko, N. (2001). *Guidelines for stated preference experiment design.* Available at: https://www.b.kobe-u.ac.jp/~sanko/pub/Sanko2001_1.pdf.
Silva, B. (2018). Carro elétrico tem consumo seis vezes mais barato que a gasolina. *Dinheiro Vivo,* 1–10.
Soyinka, T. (2019). All about using Uber in Portugal. *bePortugal.* Available at: https://beportugal.com/uber-in-portugal/
Tesla. (2020). *Tesla—Carros elétricos, painéis solares e armazenamento de energia limpa.* Available at: https://www.tesla.com/pt_pt. Accessed: January 30, 2020.
Transport and Environment. (2017). *Does sharing cars really reduce car use?* Available at: https://www.transportenvironment.org/publications/does-sharing-cars-really-reduce-car-use.
UBER. (2020). *Uber—Aumente os seus rendimentos a conduzir ou obtenha uma viagem agora.* Available at: https://www.uber.com/pt/pt-pt/. Accessed: January 30, 2020.
Verbrugg, M. W., & Wampler, C. W. (2017). On the optimal sizing of batteries for electric vehicles and the influence of fast charge. *Journal of Power Sources, 384,* 312–317.

The Shared Mobility Sector in Italy

Massimo Ciuffini, Luca Refrigeri, and Sofia Asperti

Abstract Italian shared mobility is a phenomenon that is constantly growing, from both the demand and supply side of services. Looking at it as a whole, taking into consideration all shared mobility services enabled by digital platforms, the picture is positive, and the same is true if we analyze the different services separately. Vehicle and ride-sharing services are growing in quantitative terms, demonstrating positive adaptation to the challenges emerging, case by case, in the context of Italian cities. In the second part, trends and statistics of the Italian shared mobility sector are analyzed. This analysis serves to highlight political and technical issues that must be resolved in Italy to limit the primacy of individual mobility in the advantage of shared mobility.

Keywords Shared mobility · Sustainable mobility · Italy · Transport sector · Mobility-as-a-service

1 Introduction: Mobility as a Shared Service

The shared use of a mobility service is a trait common to all forms of transport that do not involve the use of a vehicle. Therefore, traditional transport services such as train, subway, tram, bus, and taxi, as well as the so-called new shared mobility services—or innovative shared mobility—such as the bike sharing, car sharing, carpooling,[1] and other innovative services enabled by the use of digital platforms. All shared mobility services work because there is an organization (from the simplest to the most complex) that provides a mobility service and a number of subjects who make use of this service, shared vehicles, and journeys. The sharing of mobility services can take place in two different ways: in sequence, as in the case of a carpooling service or a taxi ride, or simultaneously, that is, when sharing a journey by subway or carpooling.

M. Ciuffini (✉) · L. Refrigeri · S. Asperti
Sustainable Mobility Unit, Sustainable Development Foundation, Rome, Italy
e-mail: ciuffini@susdef.it

G. Smorto and I. Vinci (eds.), *The Role of Sharing Mobility in Contemporary Cities*, UNIPA Springer Series, https://doi.org/10.1007/978-3-030-57725-4_6

Like the other traditional on-demand services such as taxis and rental with or without a driver, all shared mobility services are characterized by being available at the request of the passengers, according to itineraries and schedules established from time to time. Compared to the former, however, shared mobility services are enabled by new digital technologies. It is due to this fundamental technological revolution that some niche services have started to establish themselves as forms of mass production/consumption and that pre-existing mobility practices or services, such as hitchhiking, car rental or the same taxi services have undergone a radical transformation, evolving toward services with original features. The characteristics that distinguish shared mobility services from both scheduled and traditional on-demand services are the following:

- Reticulation—Digital platforms allow you to create faster and more effective relationships and exchanges beyond physical boundaries.
- Interactivity—Through digital platforms, users of shared mobility services not only have the opportunity to use but also to create/modify the services demanded. The real-time interaction, enabled by the digital platforms, allows continuous adaptability of contents by service providers to adapt them to users' needs.
- Collaboration—Network activates multiple forms of collaboration and coordination between individuals. The formation of a community is an element of recognition and reputation, and it represents an opportunity to enable multiple transactions, including non-commercial ones based on exchanges and gifts.
- Use of residual capacity—Shared mobility services are characterized by the ability to exploit the residual capacity concerning the use of personal vehicles. Vehicle productivity can grow in a journey—when the load factor increases, for example, thanks to the use of a carpooling platform—or on a time scale—when the time in which a vehicle is parked decreases, in particular at the roadside, thanks to a car sharing platform.
- Playfulness—The shared mobility services are designed to ensure a user experience based on not only ease of use (user-friendly) but also on play and fun.

Technological innovation makes it possible to provide shared mobility services comparable with those offered by traditional on-demand services but at more accessible costs and better performance. In the case of vehicle-sharing services, technological, and organizational innovation allows the user's ability to drive a vehicle to be combined with the possibility of renting without any interaction with the dedicated staff. As a result, vehicle-sharing services are offered at competitive prices compared to other transport/mobility services that need a driver or a network of employees to collect and return vehicles. In ride-sharing services, on the other hand, innovation not only makes it possible to multiply the possibilities of a match between supply and demand but also to reduce the unit costs of travel.

A carpooling journey, for example, is offered by one driver to one (or more) passenger, both members of the same platform, in exchange for a part of the travel expenses, an amount of money normally lower than what is requested by a transport company. Although it is still a small share of the modal split, innovative shared

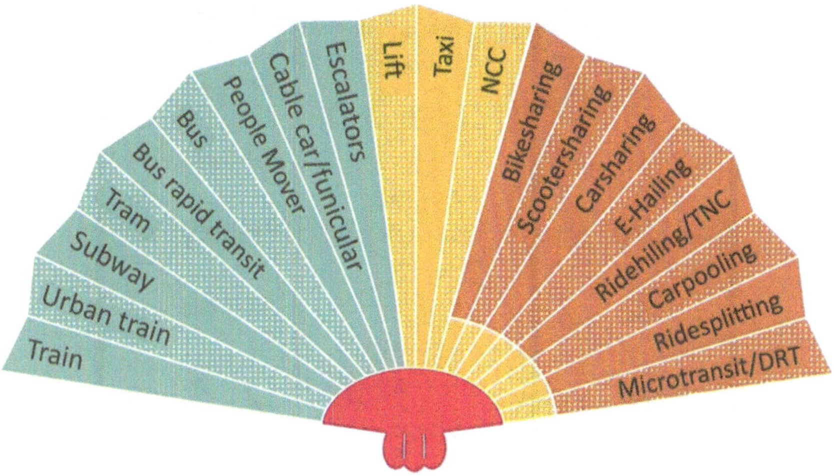

Fig. 1 "Fan" of shared mobility. *Source* Italian shared mobility platform

mobility services can be used more frequently and by a much wider audience than the traditional on-demand services, thanks to the cost reduction and the ability to meet the increasingly granular, unpredictable, and ubiquitous demand for mobility (Fig. 1).

The fact that the number of shared mobility services increases and that their performance is better than other on-demand services creates new and unprecedented opportunities for integration. This evolution is possible thanks to the availability of new digital technologies and to the multiplication of the combinations available to those who, to move, intend to access a mobility service instead of using their personal means of transport. The integration of mobility services can take place:

- Along the itinerary, that is, between the origin and the final destination of a move (intermodality);
- Over time, or in the succession of movements repeated cyclically in a day, a week, etc. (Multimode).

In intermodal or combined trips, shared mobility services increase the attractiveness of the scheduled transport services (local public transport for example) to complete the so-called first and last mile. The integration of complementary options allows new and better travel solutions that are able to compete with a door-to-door journey by personal vehicles. The commercial integration between different mobility services, and the full interoperability of the single payment systems, is achieved today with MaaS platforms. With this type of platform, consumers can buy mobility services provided by one or more operators using a single platform in a single economic transaction. The platform provides an intermodal journey planner, a booking system, real-time information to users and a single payment method for all modes of transport integrated into the platform (Fig. 2).

Fig. 2 Plan the intermodal trip. *Source* Italian shared mobility platform

The widening and enrichment of the range of shared mobility services allow individuals to use the most convenient travel solution from time to time, as an alternative to the exclusive use of their means of transport, by increasing multimodality. This condition occurs when individuals, who normally cyclically perform different types of travel during the week, use different mobility services from time to time, depending on the specific needs they intend to meet. If the range of mobility solutions available widens, it will be possible to prefer train to car, to go from the suburbs to the central areas of the city, bicycles to the subway to do shopping near the office, or carpooling to the buses to return home at night when the frequency of public transport is too low. When this condition is realized because the offer of mobility services is sufficiently large, for each movement we tend to use the service and the mode of transport in its optimal conditions.

The so-called mobility "bundles", integrated commercial mobility packages, and foster the integration between different modes of transport, even in this case, thanks to the MaaS platform development. Within these mobility bundles, there may be different combinations of services, composed according to the users' habits and needs. The different services are offered as prepaid travel minutes by different mobility services (taxi, bus, metro, carpooling, etc.) that the user can spends according to their needs, exactly like a phone plan, which includes a certain amount of voice, SMS, and data traffic (Fig. 3).

Spatial and temporal integration between all types of shared services is a key aspect both for an offer provided efficiently and to allow users to be able to reduce the use of their means of transport, up to renouncing its possession. Only the overall widening of the range of shared mobility solutions and access to an offer of integrated mobility to replace the use of the personal vehicle can achieve the objective of efficient mobility in the consumption of resources, at low emissions and which is socially inclusive.

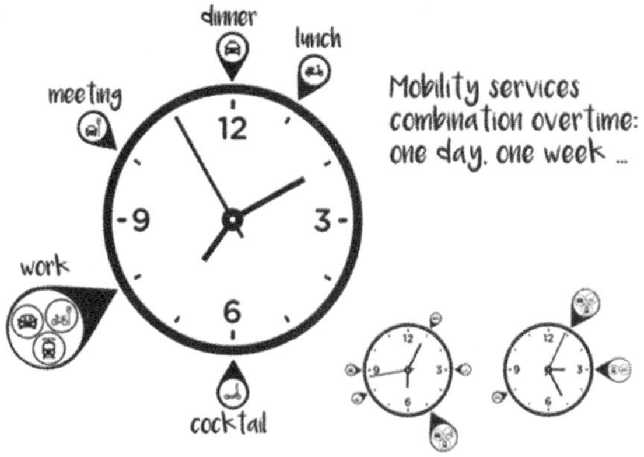

Fig. 3 Combination of mobility services over time. *Source* Italian shared mobility platform

According to the OECD[2], if the entire road traffic of a city, for the same accessibility of the territory, were to be replaced by the use of different and integrated shared mobility services, the distances of personal vehicles would be considerably reduced and, proportionally, so would all related impacts, namely from energy consumption, polluting emissions, congestion, and accidents. In addition, thanks to the much more intense use of shared vehicles compared to personal vehicles, it would be possible to reduce parking circulation and new and different use of the road space normally used for parking. The OECD/ITF model, introduced in the city of Lisbon as part of a simulation in which motorized transport is replaced by the use of three different shared mobility services (ridesplitting, microtransit, and rapid mass transport), has led to the elimination of the congestion, a one-third reduction in CO_2 emissions and a 95% reduction in public parking needs. The fleet of means of transport necessary to achieve these results is equal to only 3% of the current fleet present in the Portuguese city.

At the same time, the total number of journeys travelled by a shared vehicle is reduced, at peak times by 37%, even though each shared vehicle travels about ten times more kilometers than a personal vehicle. The life cycle of shared vehicles is much shorter due to the much longer journeys per vehicle, and this allows a faster penetration of electrification, accelerating the reduction in CO_2 emissions by urban mobility. The benefits are also social and economic, not just environmental. Congestion is reduced and the trips offered are door-to-door; what is more, general accessibility to city services for citizens increases drastically, also guaranteeing more access equity. Thanks to the high occupancy rate of vehicles, getting around is cheaper; even without public subsidies, and the cost of a city trip can drop by up to 50% compared to current conditions. Huge spaces previously dedicated to parking can be converted to improve the livability of cities (parks, wider sidewalks, or better cycle paths for instance).

It is possible to observe how the new possibility to request, book, and pay for travel is changing the way people move and interact with mobility services once again, calling into question the primacy of personal mobility. Digitization is at the heart of this revolution. The first aspect of this rapid and radical transformation is the quantity and quality of the new shared mobility services that have been emerging in recent years, enabled by digital platforms. In some cases, such as the free-floating bike sharing, these are global transformation trends. In other cases, these innovative services come from urban areas and spread everywhere, such as the so-called shared micro-mobility of which electric scooters are part. Some services reveal great potential although they have not yet had an equally disruptive claim, such as microtransit (also called DRT) or peer-to-peer vehicle-sharing.

The second aspect is that shared mobility services increase and improve, together with the opportunities to combine different services. The existence of multimodal journey planners today, and MaaS platforms in the future, open possibilities that have not yet been explored to imagine, build, and consume integrated mobility starting from a click on one's smartphone. When planning a move from home to work, as well as a long-distance journey, people consider the cost, convenience, and complexity of the entire door-to-door journey—not a single element of it. Today, this can be done much more easily than in the past because services offered by many operators and different modes of transport are combined.

The third aspect is perhaps the most revolutionary. Today, when you buy a car, you buy a "prepaid travel bundle." Often purchased in installments or by paying long-term leasing or rental fees, our car represents our guaranteed possibility to move anywhere, anytime. Analyzing the performance of all shared mobility services, while traditional services continue to ensure high capacity, speed, and scale of activity, for which they occupy an irreplaceable position in the contemporary transport landscape, innovative shared mobility services (and taxis) can offer those characteristics of accessibility, availability, flexibility, and versatility typical of the personal vehicles (Fig. 4).

If the entire range of shared mobility services is included in a "prepaid mobility services package", thanks to a coordinated offer between operators and integration in the MaaS platforms, a smartphone can be the "ignition key" of our freedom to move. The advent of digital also enables new forms of coordination between different industrial sectors. Use of digital platforms, dematerialization of transactions, and continuous connection and navigation shift from binary relationships to networks; these are only some of the new characteristics of our daily life experience. The new perception of reality pushes individuals to also desire a way of moving in physical reality that is ever closer to what happens in the virtual world.

This means that individuals are now much more oriented toward using mobility services in combination with each other than they were in the past. The main reason is that they perceive that all of this is technically possible.

Furthermore, accessing instead of owning, "being transported" instead of "driving," is something that is slowly becoming closer to the contemporary lifestyle: It is better to travel by train and be able to do other things like reading a book, watching a movie, or "chatting" with a friend, rather than keeping your hands fixed on the wheel (Fig. 5).

The future application of so-called autonomous driving certainly contributes to consolidating this trend toward the continuous transformation of the organization

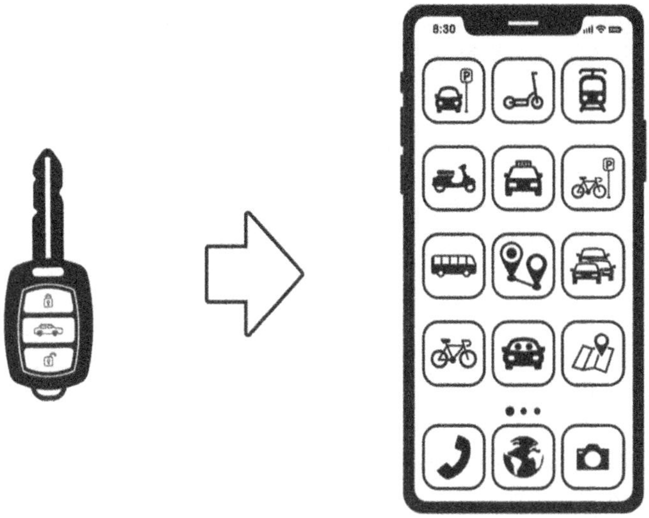

Fig. 4 Mobility as a shared service. *Source* Italian shared mobility platform

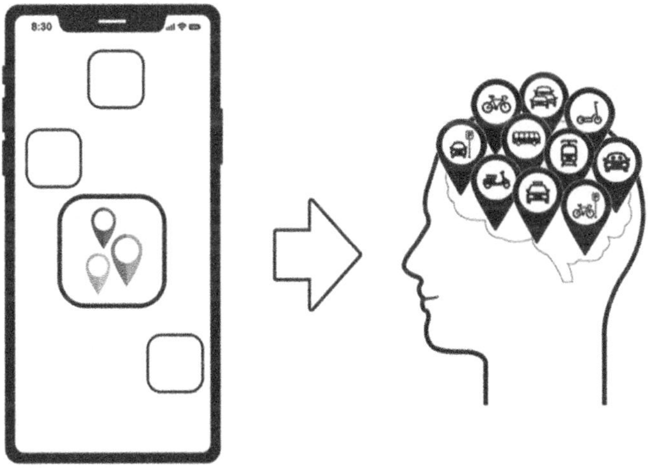

Fig. 5 MaaS and the power of idealization. *Source* Italian shared mobility platform

and consumption models of shared services, many of the differences between the services to date. Driverless vehicles will allow a radical reduction in the operating costs of some types of service as well as the possibility to offer travel solutions that are even closer to demand in terms of availability, flexibility, and scalability. Selected autonomous driving, for example, which becomes even more competitive—both in terms of price and performance—some shared services such as ride-hailing, micro-transit, and also carpooling. In reality, all these names, when a car no longer has to be driven by a driver, will completely lose their sense. What will be the difference between a taxi and carpooling from the moment a car can reach—traveling empty—the point where we called it, and then take us where we need it, without us driving it?

We are facing a new and imminent paradigm change today, considering these transformations due to the digital revolution, similar to the advent of mass motorization in the past. It is a new direction and one that challenges the primacy of personal mobility over shared mobility, to raise mobility-as-a-service over self-produced mobility.

2 How is Italian Shared Mobility Doing?

Shared mobility continues to grow in Italy, confirming itself as one of the last decades' transport innovations as well as a social and cultural phenomenon of our days. Innovative shared mobility services are seeing their data on usage grow year after year, increasing the number and type of digital platforms and the vehicles shared in Italian cities. The sector numbers testify to its progress and health, telling us how and how much the transport offer is expanding and how the demand for mobility is increasingly oriented toward alternative solutions to the use of your own mode of transport, by radically changing behavioral patterns and habits. It is enough to consider that the number of trips made by an innovative shared mobility service in 2018 was a little over 33 million according to the Italian Shared Mobility Platform's estimates, 26% more than the previous year and double the figure estimated for 2015. The number of subscriptions to the digital platforms for shared mobility services also continued to rise very rapidly, reaching 5.2 million at December 31, 2018, with an increase of 24% compared to the previous year. The demand for shared mobility is also growing, as evidenced by the data on the total number of services active in Italy, which reached 363 in 2018, 100 more services than those present in 2015, and an average growth rate of 12% per year. The number of shared vehicles also consolidated in 2018, remaining stable compared to the previous year at around forty-five thousand units and more than double compared to 2015 (Fig. 6).

The innovative nature of shared mobility, however, is not only established by the break between past and present plastically represented by the use of digital technologies, but it is also concretized above all in being the most effective tool to design the mobility of the future, at the service of more sustainable cities from an environmental and social point of view. In this sense, Italian shared mobility shows encouraging signs by trying to increasingly focus on electric and light vehicles, that are capable of moving more easily within congested cities, with less environmental impact and in synergy with the use of mass public transport to cover the first and last mile of a trip. Between 2017 and 2018, the percentage of electric vehicles out of the total number of vehicles available to users increased from 27 to 43%. Such a positive percentage change is mainly due to the boom in electric scooter sharing services that increased their fleet six times in a year. The relative share of two-wheeled

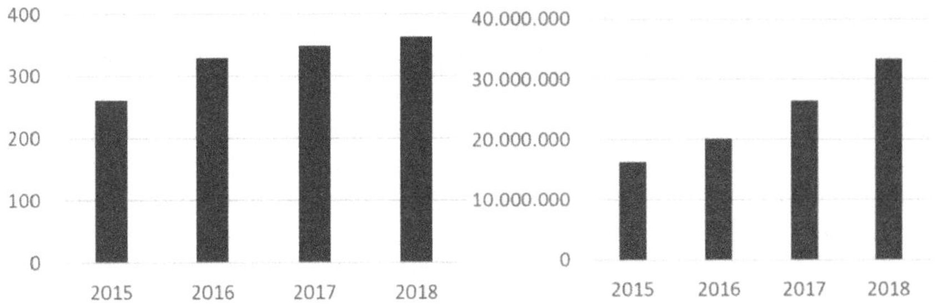

Fig. 6 Number of services in Italy (left) and number of trips made using shared mobility services (right). *Source* Italian shared mobility platform

vehicles compared to cars passed from 6% in 2017 to 22% in the following year. In addition to being more electric, the shared vehicles that circulate on our roads are also on average lighter and less cumbersome because they are designed to offer better performance in terms of consumption: the average mass of motor vehicles decreased by 17% between 2015 and 2018, opening up interesting scenarios from this point of view with the expected arrival of shared kick-scooters on the streets of Italian cities (Fig. 7).

Even car sharing, one of the traditional segments of shared mobility in Italy has become fertile ground for experimentation in recent years, in which to combine

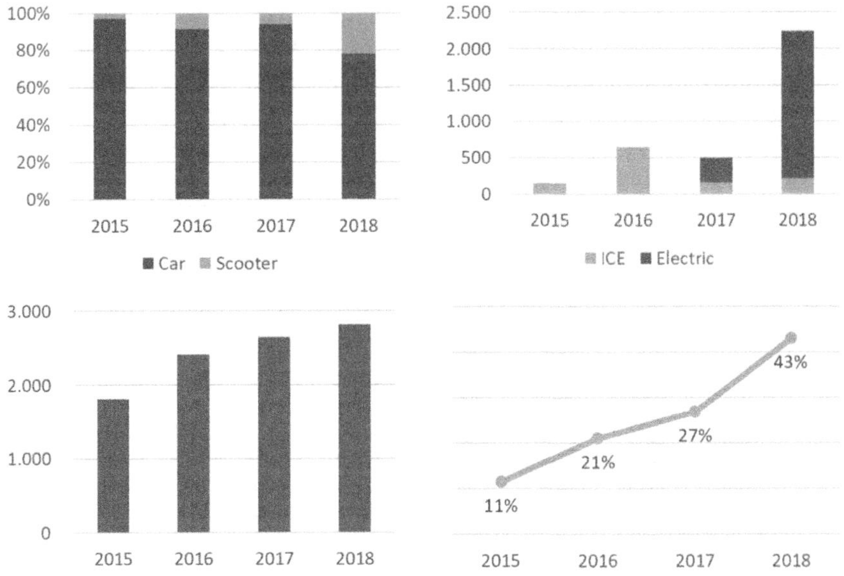

Fig. 7 Clockwise, starting from the upper left quadrant: (1) fleet composition of motor vehicles; (2) number of scooters per power supply; (3) percentage of electric vehicles out of the total (car + scooter); (4) number of shared e-bikes. *Source* Italian shared mobility platform

technological innovation in the car market, electrification, and advanced research in the digital field. Not surprisingly, in Italy, a significant change of pace in the popularity of shared mobility occurred after the arrival in 2013 of the first free-floating car sharing services on the roads of Milan and Rome. The technological revolution of the first smartphones placed at the service of the use, unconstrained and as needed, of an individual vehicle such as the car, had the merit of showing the potential of the new shared mobility services to a much wider audience than that which had already pioneered the shared mobility services. Innovation, therefore, but also consolidation of the structural data of the carpooling sector, just like in the case of free-flow services. There were a total of 1 million and 860 thousand registrations for car sharing services in Italy in 2018, of which approximately 90% for free-floating services, a share that grew by 27% compared to 2017 with an average progression of 40% in the period 2015–2018. The number of people approaching free-floating services is growing alongside the use of fleet vehicles, reaching 11.8 million trips, in line with the improvement trend of the last few years, for a total of 80 million km, twice as many as in 2015. The offer in terms of cars available for users grew less than in previous years, setting the total of free-floating cars at 6787 in 2018, proof of consolidation of services on the territory in the face of greater use of cars per day. In the last year, Turin was the city with the highest average turnover rate for free-floating fleets (6.2 trips/cars/day), ahead of Milan (5.6), Rome (4.1), and Florence (3) (Fig. 8).

Positive dimensions and perspectives are also observed for station-based car sharing, the progenitor of the Italian family of this type of vehicle-sharing service. The forms of carpooling structured into the mobility service arrived in Italy between the 90s and 2000s as a result of the Decree of the Ministry of the Environment "Interventions for sustainable mobility," issued in March 1998. The first car sharing services to start in Italy, therefore, used fixed vehicle pickup and drop-off points, systems which in some cases are still active in the area today, even in the South, with good and consolidated numbers of supply and demand. Registrations and trips are rising, the first growing by 37% in 2018 compared to the previous year and on average by 22% every year since 2015, while trips have increased by 8% compared

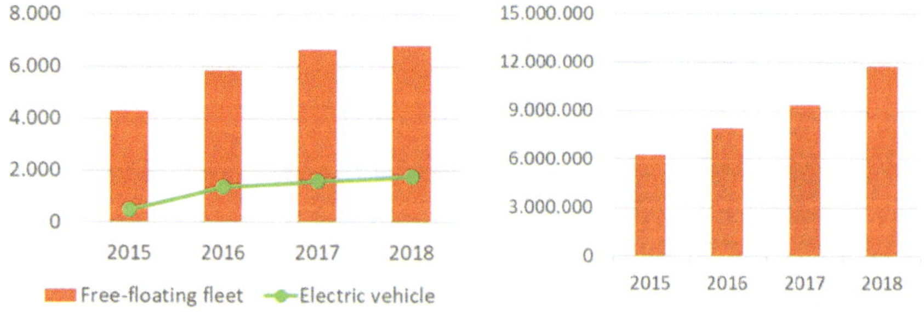

Fig. 8 Fleet (left) and number of trips (right) of free-floating car sharing. *Source* Italian shared mobility platform

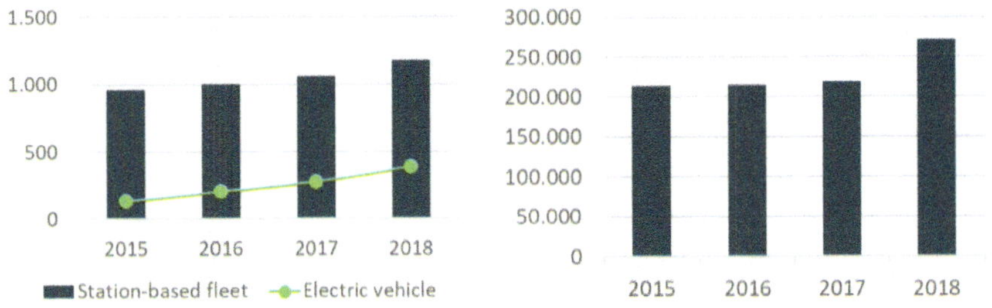

Fig. 9 Fleet (left) and number of trips (right) of station-based car sharing. *Source* Italian shared mobility platform

to 2017, arriving in the last year surveyed by the Italian Shared Mobility Platform at 270 thousand in total. Total journeys made with station-based carpooling vehicles also rose to 8.2 million kilometers in 2018 and increased by 12% compared to the previous year. With the same percentage, the number of cars in the fleet grew compared to 2017, in particular with regard to electric vehicles, which grew by 40% in 2018. The longevity of station-based carpooling services is undoubtedly the result of the adaptability and scalability of this type of service to different urban realities, but also the result of continuous research and innovation on technologies and the organization of services. Among the most interesting developments, there is undoubtedly regional carpooling which works on areas of the territory larger than the single municipality, involving more cities, and of combined systems in which the rental can also take place, limited to some areas, in free-floating mode, thanks to digital geo-refencing (Fig. 9).

With an evolutionary path very similar to car sharing services, the growth and continuous transformation of Italian bikesharing continues. Even in this case, the arrival on the roads of free-floating services toward the end of 2017 was an element of great innovation for citizens and municipal administrations, with an increase of 147% compared to 2016 in terms of bicycle sharing. After the closedown of some big free-floating services (Rome, Milan), the total amount of bikes decreased by 9% in 2018, reaching 35 thousand units, a number that includes the station-based fleet enriched with more electrical vehicles (+6% in 2018 compared to the previous year). By analyzing the number of three cities in which there are free-floating and station-based systems simultaneously, it was also possible to share the possible coexistence of the two types of bike sharing service. While on the one hand, the systems based on fixed stations pay something in terms of rentals for the inevitable overlap on the catchment area, on the other they improve in terms of subscriptions to their services, increased by 21% in 2018. Furthermore, the concerns initially related to the use of free-floating services seem to be largely reduced, in particular those related to the lack of care in the management of bicycles within the urban space. In 2019, the arrival of free-floating services in small and medium-sized cities in central Italy, and new operators with thousands of free-floating electric bicycles on the road in Rome, Turin, and Milan, highlight a strong vitality in the sector. Bike sharing has expanded

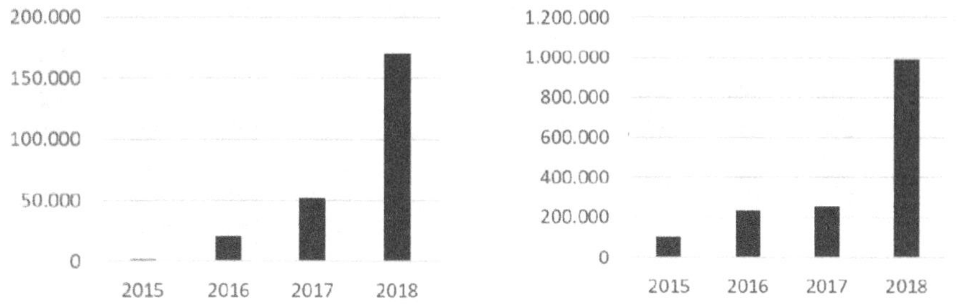

Fig. 10 Subscription (left) and number of trips (right) of scooter sharing. *Source* Italian shared mobility platform

and consolidated its offer to meet a growing demand for small, fast, and practical vehicles to travel around the city.

The scooter sharing sector performances confirm this trend looking at 2018 figures. The progression that the sector has achieved in the last year is undoubtedly the best of the Italian shared mobility sectors, with 2240 vehicles on 31 December 2018 of which 90% electric. The national fleet quadrupled and the expansion of services supports an equally strong increase in demand: Registrations in 2018 are 230% more than in 2017, while the number of as trips foresees the share of 1 million (+285%), with rotation rates marking maximum peaks of 4 trips per day per vehicle. Even in scooter sharing, it is clear that electrification and a loss of size (mass and power) of the vehicles will be the ingredients for building business models and services known by the public which, in this specific case, are the perfect mobility solutions for moving over medium distances—long urban areas and few parking problems once they have arrived at their destination. The trend of sharing lighter and electric vehicles, therefore, becomes an important feature of the shared mobility in Italy. This is confirmed by observing the two-wheel segment, which in 2019 leaped forward with the advent of kick-scooters in sharing and the tendency, looking at the supply side, to offer both micro-mobility devices and e-bikes (Fig. 10).

The sharing economy involves one of the most characteristic phenomena in the context of the contemporary economic-productive organization of our societies. The daily use of social platforms and the multiplication of virtual communities able to accommodate a practically infinite number of participants, offer the conditions for the future development of new types of vehicle-sharing services. Less popular in Italy, but alternative to free-floating and station-based systems, are the peer-to-peer services. They are based on personal car loans between members (whether they are private citizens, long-term rental companies, long-term parking terminals, or other subjects) using a digital platform that organizes the service and fosters the match between supply and demand. In Italy and everywhere, there are already activities that offer traditional rental services between individuals (Consumer-2-Consumer) or in some cases, they also involve corporate fleets (Business-2-Business-2-Consumer). From this point of view, the synergies between P2P carpooling and long-term rental models are very interesting. Other kinds of peer-to-peer services, activated in Italy

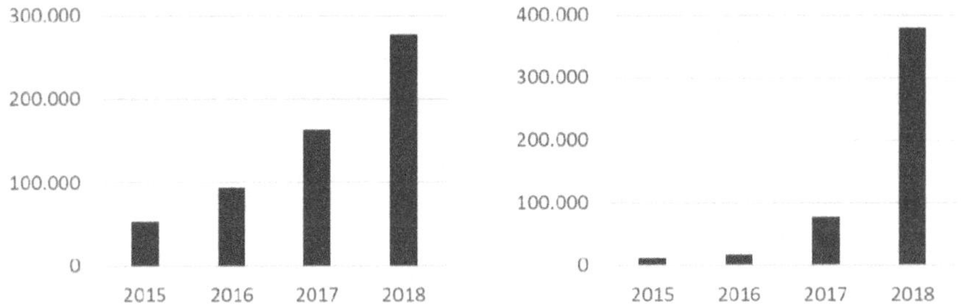

Fig. 11 Subscription (left) and number of trips (right) of corporate carpooling services. *Source* Italian shared mobility platform

between 2018 and 2019, put at the center of the exchange not only cars but also vehicles intended for different uses, such as campers and caravans. Looking at the more consolidated European market data, it is possible to predict that in the future peer-to-peer sharing may represent an important alternative to the mobility demand also in Italy.

Positive data can also be highlighted for ride-sharing services, the class of innovative shared mobility that includes carpooling, e-hail, ride-hailing, ridesplitting, microtransit, or demand-responsive transit (DRT). The number of subscriptions to platforms for sharing extra-urban travel grew by 15% between 2017 and 2018, exceeding 2.8 million in the last year, for a total offer of 1.5 million rides. Also with regard to corporate carpooling, in recent years there has been strong growth in registrations, on average 75% per year since 2015, which foresees an increase of 277 thousand at the end of 2018. Growth in subscribers goes hand in hand with growth in the number of shared trips, which also increases, with growth rates of 800% from one year to the next. The fact that awareness of the issue of shared and sustainable mobility has increased even within Italian companies is evidenced by the increasingly frequent opportunities for cooperation between managers and workers, who together design incentive and reward plans for the training in equipment, increases in shared steps, and changing of individual mobility habits (Fig. 11).

Digital services for booking taxi rides are one of the most dynamic shared mobility sectors today, and potentially able to intercept a very large share of mobility demand. Just think of the widespread use of the taxi service in Italy, where it is present in all provincial capitals with more than 23 thousand licenses currently active. Leading the ranking of the number of licenses per 1000 inhabitants is Milan with 36 licenses, followed by Rome with 27, and Naples with 24, while further behind are Florence, Turin, and Bologna with 17 licenses per thousand inhabitants. Depending on the regulation of the current market, this type of service takes different forms. In Italy, for example, those who have a taxi license can offer a street service also through a digital e-hail platform but always within the existing regulatory framework (timetables, rates, etc.). Same thing for NCC (car rental with driver) operators, who instead can use ride-hailing platforms. The ridesplitting service also provides for the possibility of training crews of multiple users who coordinate to share the journey between an origin and a predetermined destination. Trying to outline a synthetic picture of the offer, there are three types of e-hail digital platforms currently active on the market in Italy, which differ in operator/manager and type of service offered to taxi drivers: (1) platforms for consortia of cooperatives, (2) platforms for taxi cooperatives, (3) platforms for taxi drivers. According to the most recent data collected by the observatory and updated in the first months of 2019, there are 120 cities where one or more platforms operate simultaneously, while the rides booked via digital application were 3.1 million at December 31, 2018, considering only the largest player of the three categories listed above.

One of the crucial and booming segments in Italian shared mobility is that of digital platforms for travel planning through local public transport and the aggregation of shared mobility services. Especially in the use of collective modes such as public transport, new requirements in demand are perfectly recognizable today, alongside the traditional ones, such as operation, reliability, safety, and cleanliness. Greater customization of services, for example, or maximum widening of multimodality in trip planning, single ticketing, real-time information updates on the trip, and possible reprogramming of the trip as needed, just to name a few. Today, it is thus possible to observe a growing number of technology companies and start-ups that identify the new needs of Italian passengers of shared mobility and who, through their digital applications, enter the sector by questioning habits and practices consolidated for decades, attracted firstly, by the great potential that the daily travel market offers. In Italy, the number of cities in which digital travel planning services with LPT and vehicle-sharing platform management is accessible has increased further: 47 in 2018 compared to 43 in 2017, enabling 40 services (7 services more than the previous year), including micro-mobility services (scooters) in Milan and Florence. The start up in Turin of the first MaaS pilot project called Living Lab MaaS is also worth mentioning, which aims to create a mobility ecosystem involving TPL, bikesharing, scootersharing, and e-hailing platforms.

3 Dissemination of Services and New Development Perspectives

On a territorial distribution level, free-floating carpooling continues to be a phenomenon exclusively linked to the large cities in the center and North of Italy. Milan with 22 cars per 10,000 inhabitants remains the city with the highest offer of free-floating vehicles in Italy, followed by Florence (13), Bologna (9), Turin (8), and then Rome (7). The territorial coverage of station-based carpooling is wider in terms of cities reached by services, thanks also to the consolidated experience of regional northern carsharing and those inaugurated in 2018 in Salento and Sardinia in the provinces of Lecce and Sassari. Cagliari is the city with the highest offer in terms of cars per inhabitant, followed by Palermo, Turin, Venice, and Milan.

The diffusion of free-floating bikesharing services, as in the case of shared cars, remains confined exclusively to the municipalities of the northern regions except for Florence, first in the offer ranking of vehicles with more than 10 bicycles per 1000 inhabitants, followed by Milan and Bologna with values around 6 bikes/1000 inhabitants. The situation is different for station-based bikesharing services that are present in the southern regions, but only with services of less than 100 bicycles. No city in the south has larger bikesharing systems except the one active in Palermo with 400 bicycles. Milan, on the other hand, is the city with the highest offer per inhabitant, 3.5 fixed station bikes per 1000 inhabitants.

The spread of scooter sharing services is also still limited to only three major cities: Milan, Rome, and Turin. Milan is the city with more services (5) and more scooters per inhabitant (10 per 10,000 inhabitants), followed by Rome with 2 services and 2.5 scooters per 10,000 inhabitants, and Turin with 1 service and 1, 7 vehicles per 10,000 inhabitants.

Near the undoubtedly positive numbers of Italian shared mobility, there are other important parameters for determining the situation of shared mobility in our country. One of these derives from the analysis of the presence of services in the area and the type of offer present in the various geographical areas, to which the Italian shared mobility platform pays attention in its annual Report. What emerges from the analysis conducted in 2018 on a sample of 34 Italian cities made up of regional capitals, metropolitan cities and cities with more than 150 thousand inhabitants is a general polarization in the diffusion of shared mobility services, with a large imbalance toward northern regions and, for free-floating services, a marked imbalance in favor of large cities.

If on the one hand traditional shared mobility services such as local public transport and taxi services are not lacking in any of the cities observed, only 2 cities in the south can boast the presence of shared mobility services that are currently active: Palermo and Cagliari, where there are carpooling and bike sharing services (with more than 100 bikes). About the presence of services in the south, none of the cities in the analyzed sample has a free-floating carpooling service (even if the carpooling from Palermo and Cagliari provide in some specific areas the possibility of pick-up and drop-off outside the stations), a free-flow bike sharing service, or a scooter sharing service.

Palermo and Cagliari, therefore, represent good practices for the dissemination of services in the South, but Bologna also provides positive indications regarding future developments in the sector. The Emilian capital is the example of a medium-sized city that has inaugurated a new season of shared mobility in the last two years, with free-floating carpooling and bike sharing services, including electric ones, overcoming the main ones with their planning and organization technical barriers related to the implementation of free-flow services in territories of this size.

Other similar examples could be made in a sector such as shared mobility that demonstrates dynamism and innovation, especially in its organizational models, but what seems clear is that there is a widespread awareness by citizens and institutions (on a municipal scale more than national) on the role that cities are called to play today. Cities must be protagonists in the process of transforming urban mobility to reduce the weight of personal cars, reduce vehicle speed in the city, increase space for less impactful and lighter modes, and clear the streets of the big cars parked there. In this direction, for the promotion of a regulated, harmonious and widespread growth of shared mobility services, it is necessary to establish a set of uniform rules and instruments at the national level for the activation, operation, and monitoring of shared mobility services, able to regulate the negative aspects and encourage the best ones.

3.1 Priority Lines of Intervention

Remove obstacles to the operation of some innovative shared mobility services currently absent on the italian market

Nowadays, car, bike, and scooter sharing services operate within a framework of rules that did not expressly provide for their existence but which did not prevent their development. This condition also applies to most carpooling services and, in part, to e-hailing services. This does not happen for the ridesplitting and micro-transit/DRT services, currently not present in the Italian shared mobility landscape. Urban carpooling services also suffer from the undefined regulatory framework, and some services, even after excellent feedback in terms of use, have been suspended for regulatory reasons.

Regulate the use of public space and roadways

In the context of the development of sustainable urban mobility, it is necessary to reallocate the public space of roadways (a scarce resource that belongs to everyone) according to the principles of equity, efficiency, and environmental sustainability. This can be done through regulatory measures (LTZ, low emission zones, Zone 30, pedestrian or pedestrian priority zones, parking regulation, etc.), tax measures (parking fees, tolls for access to city areas and use of road infrastructures, etc.) and through the public spaces designed for the traffic of vehicles and pedestrians.

Guarantee a competitive advantage to innovative shared mobility services on a par with traditional shared mobility services

To guarantee the basic framework for an efficient and equitable allocation of public space, to encourage the growth and diffusion of innovative shared mobility services, local authorities must be able to:

- reserve parking spaces for vehicles used for shared mobility services (on the road and in car parks close to the large poles of attraction for urban mobility, in particular, railway stations and rapid mass transport), with a specific space reserved for electric vehicles;
- allocate spaces for stopping and collecting passengers for ride-sharing services;
- allow transit in the lanes reserved for the circulation of vehicles used for public transport services and access to areas with limited traffic or tolls, with reduced rates, if compatible with existing traffic flows.

Extend the economic incentives reserved for other shared mobility services to innovative shared mobility services

Economic incentives adopted for local public transport services and non-scheduled public services must be extended to innovative shared mobility services. For example, it is necessary to equate the facilitated tax regimes of all operators of shared mobility services, promote incentive tools such as energy-efficiency certificates (TEE or "white certificates"), and extend the use of innovative shared mobility services to all tax concessions today aimed at users of local public transport.

Establish minimum but uniform rules at national level

For a regulated, harmonious, and widespread growth of shared mobility services, it is necessary to define a set of uniform rules and instruments at the national level for the activation, operation, and monitoring of shared mobility services. The first step in this direction is the definition of guidelines for the assignment of shared mobility services throughout the national territory. This can facilitate local authorities/mobility agencies' tasks and identify the minimum content, as regards minimum standards of quality to protect the customer, minimum monitoring, and reporting obligations toward the granting bodies, minimum requirements for interoperability, and legal frameworks to be chosen for management.

Support innovative shared mobility services with public resources

Local communities must be able to indistinctly subsidize all shared mobility services not only local public transport services, if this meets efficiency criteria and ensures tangible benefits for the community such as fair accessibility of the territory and the reduction of the impacts of mobility. The first form of integration that must be implemented between services is to integrate the various forms of public funding to achieve the overall sustainability objectives of the transport system.

Improve high-capacity shared mobility services

To increase the demand for shared mobility as a whole, homogeneous fast and high-capacity shared transport services (trains, subways, tramways, reserved and high-frequency buses) must grow and improve throughout the country. They represent the backbone of the entire shared transport system. Growth must take place homogeneously throughout the national territory, not only in large cities and not only in the most developed areas of the country. Speed, capacity, and efficient use of the space by scheduled shared mobility services are criteria that can assert themselves in any urban context, according to a gradient function of the geographical size, population density, and compactness of the building.

Create a widespread network of mobility hubs

To allow integration between mobility services and between different modes of transport, it is necessary to create a hub for sustainable mobility at different scales, according to the different territorial areas and according to the different types of services to be connected. In urban areas, mass rapid transit stations, as nodal points of the entire shared mobility system, must be the subject of investment policy to radically update their internal and external configuration and favor the exchange between mobility as well as between different modes of transport. No less important are the hubs dedicated to the exchange of lower-capacity mobility services, which serve modest volumes of traffic but are more widespread in the peri-urban or rural area.

Building a national digital ecosystem

It is necessary to benefit from reliable and updated data on how people and vehicles move in order to take informed decisions on the use of physical infrastructures, to regulate the transport market, and to improve the quality of the mobility services offered to citizens. For this scope, it is important to build an accessible national digital ecosystem in which mobility providers share data and related APIs according to shared technological standards. This national digital ecosystem can create the conditions for developing innovative mobility services, to allow the development of integration platforms for mobility, encourage competition, and avoid monopolistic positions in the digital age.

Notes

1 For the definitions of services adopted by the National Sharing Mobility Observatory, see "Glossary" in the 3rd National Report on Sharing Mobility downloadable from the website: www.obsatoriosharingmobility.it.

2 ITF (2016), Shared Mobility: Innovation for Liveable Cities, ITF (2017), Shared Mobility Simulations for Helsinki e ITF (2017), 5 Shared Mobility Simulations for Auckland.

The manufacturer's authorised representative in the EU is Springer Nature Customer Service Centre GmbH, Europaplatz 3, 69115 Heidelberg, Germany. If you have any concerns regarding our products, please contact ProductSafety@springernature.com

Printed and bound by CPI Group (UK) Ltd, Croydon, CR0 4YY
30/09/2026
02225472-0015